THANK GOODNESS OPPOSITES ATTRACT ...

She means:
abandon *n.* A state of ecstasy one reads about: "Why don't we make love with abandon?" Response: "With a what?"

He means:
abandon *v.* To produce a painful state in another simply by going where you want to go: "How could you abandon me? Response: "Uh, I was hungry."

busy *adj.* Utterly swamped unless someone special calls.

busy *adj.* Utterly swamped unless someone special dies.

call *n.* A phone call; an imitation of caring; a proclamation of desire or friendship.

call *v.* What you should do a few days after fooling around if you want to do it again.

HE MEANT/SHE MEANT

She: "It's about male-female communication. We finally explain the whole thing. The purpose is to reach a new, deeper, more ecstatic level of understanding between the sexes."

He: "It's about 224 pages."

JENNY LYN BADER has strong feelings of empathy for people she has never met, feels just terrible about things that could not possibly be her fault, and always wears heels. She is a writer living in New York City whose work has been included in *Next: Young American Writers on the New Generation* (Norton), *Who We Are* (St. Martin's), and other anthologies. She is also a member playwright at The New Group and a contributor to the MSN Serial Web drama @watercooler.

BILL BRAZELL got his ideas of men from playing Little League baseball, growing up with an Air Force dad, and counseling adolescents in a mental hospital. He is familiar with the underpaid world of internships at *Wired* magazine, as well as phone soliciting, table waiting, and Easter bunny photography. He would like to become familiar with an overpaid world that does not require neckties. He lives in Berkeley, California.

HE Meant
SHE Meant

THE DEFINITIVE MALE/FEMALE DICTIONARY

JENNY LYN BADER and BILL BRAZELL

WARNER BOOKS

A Time Warner Company

WARNER BOOKS EDITION

Copyright © 1997 by Jenny Lyn Bader and Bill Brazell
All rights reserved.

Cover design and illustration by Jon Valk

Warner Books, Inc.
1271 Avenue of the Americas
New York, NY 10020

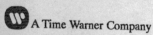 A Time Warner Company

Visit our Web site at
http://warnerbooks.com

Printed in the United States of America

First Printing: December, 1997

10 9 8 7 6 5 4 3 2 1

ACKNOWLEDGMENTS

Thanks to our editors at Warner—Jamie Raab and Airié Dekidjiev—and to our agent Joy Harris for making this happen. Thanks too to Ambrose Bierce, Paul Chung, Harry Stein, Rob McQuilkin, Eric Liu, Laura Stulman, Dave Barry, Warren Farrell, Robert Wright and Dr. Samuel Johnson. And to Jessica Avery, Jennifer Gibbs, Henning Gutmann, Dawn Clifton, Erik Passoja, Chris Linskey, Patty Ruze, Christine Reilly, Ayesha Rook, Mitch Ikuta, Yvette Doss, Katharine Lee, Mary-Claire Bachechi, Damon Hack, Karla Galdamez, Julian Sheppard, John & Amy, Michael Stroh, Wendy Joy, Mary Ann, Karen, Colin, Uncle Dick, Nana Brazell, the late Bernard P. Moynahan, Sam Williams, J. Clifford Hobbins, and Sister Mary Louise, PBVM.

This book is dedicated to our parents, with love. They managed to raise us without the benefit of a male-female dictionary, for which we are grateful. And baffled.

PREFACE

You ask what a nice girl will do?
She won't give an inch, but she won't say no.
                    —Marcus Valerius Martialis (ca. AD 40–140)

THE EVERLASTING YES, NO, MAYBE

It happens to all of us, sometimes gradually, sometimes all of a sudden. I can remember when it happened to me—the moment it struck me that men and women really are different, but in ways that defy expectations.

I had just helped a friend give a big party. More women than men said they planned to show up. A lot of men hedged or said they probably couldn't make it. But on the night itself: Surprise. There were many more men. We tried to figure out what had happened.

I realized that when men say no, they mean maybe; and when women say yes, they mean no.

Party-throwers, would-be rapists, testing services, encyclopedia salesmen, court stenographers, telephone pollsters, and amorous types should take note.

With the possible exception of Nancy Reagan, women don't adore just saying no. Women accused of "leading on" men also "lead on" their female friends by promising to show up—which stems from an impulse to please, not a desire to tease.

Men, on the other hand, do not accept invitations or agree to demands easily. They feel that doing so would make them seem like pushovers, losers in the power games we play. Men enjoy one-upmanship. Of course "one-upwomanship" is possible, but it's not preferred.

Women prefer to avoid antagonizing anybody, be they man, woman, child, or small furry animal. That's why agreeable females dominate the "yes" lists of inexperienced party-givers. That's why confused men go home alone from what seemed to them like a good date. That's why women understood perfectly that Anita Hill, whatever demons may have been haunting her at the time, maintained contact with Clarence Thomas.

Concerned Supreme Court nominees need only refer to the precedent set in the last scene of Henrik Ibsen's *Hedda Gabler*, where Hedda admits, "I am in your power, Judge Brack. You have me at your beck and call, from this time forward." Then she shoots herself in the head. That's the archetypal nineteenth-century woman saying "Yes" and meaning "You revolt me, you pig."

A century later, mixed signals are still going strong. The political scene has spawned some classic "no-means-maybe" men. When Ross Perot said he didn't want to run for president, he meant maybe he would if a grassroots movement mysteriously started sprouting up around him. When Bill Clinton said he hadn't avoided the draft, he meant maybe he had, it depends what you mean by avoiding. When George Bush said No New Taxes, he meant Maybe New Taxes.

Everybody knows to watch out for the extremes; if some guy tells you he's not planning to annex the Sudetenland, you can figure that maybe he is. But what if we had a healthier dose of suspicion for everyday denials and affirmations? It could result in better political and cocktail parties.

Just think of the predictive powers we could acquire. When Jim Baker said he had no intention of getting involved in a Middle Eastern territorial dispute, we could have taken the gender gulf into account and understood that the Gulf War was on its way. Kiefer Sutherland could have been spared undue embarrassment if he had only realized that when Julia Roberts said yes to his hand in marriage she meant no. The Secretary of State and the starlet of the hour both spoke with the best of intentions, but deep down, beneath that attractive outer layer of sanctions, each had profound reservations that would eventually astonish an expectant nation.

BEYOND STEREOTYPES

Friends nodded with recognition upon hearing about this saga of yes-no-maybe. It went against the no-means-yes stereotype, but it rang true.

I think that's often the case: while the majority of stereotypical differences between men and women can be proven false, real differences are alive and well, and pretty funny.

Deeper differences.

Women like to survey the past, men like to survey the future. Women are fond of remembering, men of forgetting. Women weigh, men measure. We thrive on surprises, they plot their course. We want the freedom to wonder, they want the freedom to wander. We enjoy people-watching; they enjoy car-watching. We discuss specifics to illuminate the general; they talk about the general to understand specifics.

But most of all, we have different ways of expressing ourselves. Even in arenas where we are similar or identical, we have different ways of saying the same darn thing. We are taught these different languages in our peer groups.

Misunderstandings arise when we attempt to say the same thing in different words but end up saying conflicting things by accident.

METHODOLOGY: HOW WE DID IT

After airing my theory of yes-no-maybe, I was approached about writing this book. I scoured the country for a man insensitive enough to have male feelings but sensitive enough to write them down. I located Bill in Albuquerque. He immediately understood.

Coincidentally, Bill had also come to terms with male and female difference. He had been formulating the theory of the Smart Bimbo, which he will describe later in detail. We felt we could end the frustration of the whole you-don't-understand-and-you-live-on-another-planet thing. To create a foreign language lexicon—except instead of English-Swahili it would be Male-Female. But how?

We decided to make lists of words to define, go to opposite ends of the country, and not speak to each other. This worked for a time. Ironically enough, we began to have fights. *(See Appendix I: The Arguments.)*

Very male-female fights. *(See Appendix II: The Correspondence.)*

We don't fight much now, and when we do, we know why. Not only because we don't have to fight about writing the dictionary anymore, but because it explained stuff to us.

We hope it does the same for you.

Men and women alike seek love, and treasure those times our common humanity rises above difference and we can finally understand what in God's name the other person is saying.

To an era of perfect communication, this book is dedicated.

—JLB

FEMALE WORDS

While men were taught to be cool, women were taught to be nice.

We'll be nice to anyone, no matter how demented or out to get us. Throughout history, we've agreed to wear absurd corsets and absurder shoes to make guys happy. We've gotten to think of their body hair as riveting so we won't have to ask them to shave it for us.

Kidnapping statistics show that little girls will follow a complete stranger just about anywhere. Grown women will marry the prison guard who tortured them or the boyfriend who forced them to watch seven-hour documentaries in Swedish.

Women will stay on the phone for hours giving strategic advice if one of our friends is in love with a colossal idiot. We'll say encouraging things about The Idiot until she finally sees the light, then when she's ready we'll tell her what we really thought of him.

Television bitches are so popular because they are so outlandish. No one told them they had to be nice, so we look on in admiration as they destroy innocent bystanders. Many of us wish we could be more like prime-time vixens and say the cruelest thing that comes to mind at any given moment. Instead we can barely think of a cruel thing to say until the conversation is already over.

Women love to talk about relationships. We'll dissect romantic possibilities to whomever will listen: parents, pets, plants, a passing mirror. It's just our way of feeling in charge of our lives before an actual relationship puts our hearts in charge.

Women care a lot about words. While a man is likely to notice if you use a word wrong, a woman will notice if you use the wrong word.

But we like the right words, used right. We like them a lot.

MALE WORDS

Every pipsqueak knows it's not manly to care about words. In fact, it's not even good to say "manly" unless you're Laura Ingalls. But it's often kind to explain things, and even the least couth brute wants to help women experience superiority. As by letting them say "Now I understand—male bonding!", or whatever other such comment escapes the lips of a young woman trying to understand a collective effort to move a piano down an escalator. By saying "male bonding" in her own cute way, the woman is able to display Superior Intellect and Human Insight, which display will serve as her contribution to moving the piano. Men know these things, but we really don't mind, since if we move one piano we earn at least one Sunday in front of the TV. Women get to be superior, men get to watch TV, everything's cool.

It was not always so. During the 1970s, men like Alan Alda and Phil Donahue were lionized for their ability to talk to women and still make piles of money. Everywhere, men panicked. Some, terrified, thought that if they could make still more money, they might not be hassled to talk. Others thought the talking must be key—since that's what women were saying on the talk shows and at home—and majored in subjects like Psychology and Women's Studies. Those poor suckers were left in the dust during the eighties, as rich ogre types like Donald Trump got all the babes by saying a few key words, like: "Sure I took all the risks and made this dough by working every day since I was ten, but after a few afternoons of exercise, shopping, and makeup, you're superior to me!"

This was a great discovery, better than a hundred Gloria Steinem videos. Men everywhere rushed to assert the superiority of women, hoping that if they *said* it enough, they wouldn't need to prove it.

This worked for a time. But then women seemed to feel

A

abandon *n.* a state of ecstasy one reads about: *"Why don't we make love with abandon?"* Response: *"With a what?"*

abhor *v.* to loathe, due to bad associations. *Anne had abhorred the ballet ever since she learned that Lloyd's wife had been a dancer.*

abstract *n.* the theoretical idea of something. *Melinda loved Dave in the abstract, but in reality he drove her crazy.*

abusive *adj.* a quality found in certain otherwise irresistible, deep-voiced, fabulous men.

accessorize *v.* to wear the right handbag and the correct amount of glitter for a given occasion.

accident-prone *adj.* suicidal, without the guts to say so.

accommodation *n.* acting respectfully toward those whom you cannot beat up.

accuse *v.* to call someone else a sinner, so that your own sin seems reasonable by comparison. *When he saw her smile at the checkout boy, Lloyd accused Jan of adultery.*

ache *n.* chronic pain you don't discuss. Acute pain, like a compound fracture, you may mention, at least to your doctor. But a bruised thigh, for example, or a broken heart, should not be shared.

acknowledge *v.* to give credit where it is due. A hateful process.

acquaintance *n.* someone whose funeral you don't have to attend.

acquiesce *v.* to pretend you don't really prefer to have your way.

action *n.* better than words. 'Nuff said.

actualized *v.* a fancy word that could mean just about anything. If someone uses it, demand clarification.

addle *v.* to confuse, as by a good combination of punches.

admire *v.* to recognize that someone else has a quality you lack, and feel good about them, anyway. *Lloyd admired the way Joe Montana threw the football and got back up from being tackled. He also admired the way Cindy Crawford stood still.*

admit *v.* to tell yourself or others the truth after a period of denial. *Melinda admitted to Robert that she minded that he didn't mind being an undertaker.*

adolescence *n.* the teenage years, spent doing homework, insulting your parents, finding a prom date, and growing breasts. *In trigonometry one day during adolescence, Suzanne told Babs she had grown four bra sizes overnight. Luckily they were studying parabolas, so the girls could sketch them freely.*

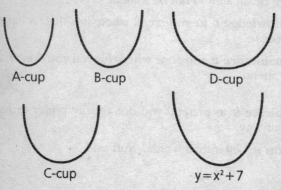

A-cup   B-cup   D-cup

C-cup $y = x^2 + 7$

advantage *n.* inherent superiority, involving excess amounts of knowledge or cleavage.

adventure *n.* an outing that can be reckless and fun, provided one brings along enough traveler's checks, first-aid kits, and contraceptives.

adversity *n.* when fate roughs you up. An opportunity to persevere.

admit *v.* **1.** to allow someone to enter. *Robert bought flowers, hoping they would induce Melinda to admit him.* **2.** to allow blame to enter. *But he knew Melinda would never admit him, if he admitted how often he still played with the late Maria.* **3.** to allow fear to enter: *Whatever happened, he couldn't admit to himself how much he liked Melinda—because unlike Maria, Melinda could leave.*

adolescence *n.* when guys find out who they are: cool, or not. The result of this time determines who you can date. *Tony quietly believed that if his adolescence had run two more years, he could have become cool.*

advantage *n.* a feature that will let you win. *Robert believed a Porsche would give him a greater advantage with women than would three years of psychotherapy.*

adventure *n.* a risk-taking act, often resulting in increased blood pressure until the act is over. *Robert found that evading commitment while maintaining sex was always an adventure.*

adversity *n.* hardship. According to Victor Hugo, "Adversity makes men. Prosperity makes monsters." Of course, prosperity also brings babes.

aerobics *n.* a great way to lose weight while indulging your secret penchant for leopard print leotards.

afford *v.* to have so much of something that you can give it away freely. *Melinda could only afford to take an hour off from work to break up with Robert.*

afterglow *n.* the light that remains in the sky after a good sunset, or in the soul after a momentous experience. Sometimes the afterglow is even better than the experience.

aftermath *n.* when you can finally see an event with stunning clarity because it is over. *In the aftermath of Robert, Melinda realized there shouldn't have been a beforemath.*

afterthought *n.* an otherwise flattering gesture that can only be construed as insulting because it comes too late.

aggressive *adj.* capable of starting a conversation or a war.

agoraphobic *n.* a bad shopping companion; a cheap date. This word comes from the ancient Greek term for fear of malls.

airhead *n.* an individual lacking mental ability. Male airheads are known as "dolts." For reasons unknown to science, dumb men breathe too little, while dumb women breathe too much, giving them an airy quality.

album *n.* **1.** a collection of songs that can be broken if the need arises. **2.** a book of photos where you store memories of events, preferably with captions, to prove to yourself that they really happened.

aerobics *n.* like cheerleading, with better music. Good to watch during breaks in weight-lifting. Reminds you of why you lift.

afford *v.* to be able to pay for a thing—and thus for its maintenance and repair, theft and collision insurance, and so on. *Steve could afford a date, but not a relationship.*

afterglow *n.* Mmmmmm. That was great. Love you, too, baby, you know I do . . . good night.

aftermath *n.* a disaster's denouement. The word you use later, when describing the way you couldn't stand the sight of the person with whom you just exchanged fluids.

afterthought *n.* the idea that occurs to you when your narcissism has relaxed enough to let your conscience speak. *Three weeks later, Robert called to say, "Hey, Melinda—here's an afterthought: I had a really nice time."*

aggressive *adj.* capable of going for what you want, despite the quailing fear that you will not only fail to get it, but will also be humiliated for trying.

agoraphobic *n.* what you are called by a former psychology major who can't get you to accompany her to Bloomingdale's for ten lousy minutes.

airhead *n.* someone not smart enough to know she's being seduced.

album *n.* **1.** a style of presenting music, playable on a turntable. Now greatly in decline. **2.** a good thing to pretend you want a date to show you. You get to sit close, while she narrates a book filled with photos of her having fun with other men.

alliance *n.* a social or political agreement to get along for the time being even if you secretly hate each other.

alone *adj.* when no one who understands you is around.

alopecia *n.* hair loss. *Anne sometimes felt that Lloyd was alopecic and trying to overcompensate.*

Amazon *n.* a woman warrior who owns a good suit of armor and lives without men but can beat them up if they ever drop in. Mythical but entirely possible.

ambition *n.* an aspiration, best unmentioned. Women once set their ambitions aside for men. Now we set them aside in polite conversation.

anaclisis *n.* libidinal/emotional attachment especially on love object based on resemblance to early childhood protective figures. *Anne wondered if her relationship with Lloyd was too anaclitic; he reminded her a great deal of her favorite uncle, and was in fact old enough to be her favorite uncle.*

angelology *n.* the study of angels, fueled by the hope that everyone we know is really a transcendent being underneath, with little wings and a halo.

angry *adj.* how men think women are feeling when they're having an emotion of any kind.

angst *n.* intense anxiety; dread. Can be an attractive quality if the person also has an accent.

anniversary *n.* an event that one can fill with meaning if one remembers when it is.

apologize *v.* to indicate that a predicament is your fault so that the guilty party will admit it was theirs.

alliance *n.* a lofty word for "selfishness, multiplied."

alone *adj.* when no one is around.

alopecia *n.* the loss of hair on one's upper head. A sign of virility, according to those who suffer it.

Amazon *n.* **1.** *Archaic.* a woman who cut off her breast in order to shoot straight. **2.** today, a woman who would sacrifice her femininity to her ambition. Amazons are often admired—by each other.

ambition *n.* what it takes to get ahead; the jockey on your back. As with genital endowment, it's charming if you seem reluctant to show your ambition. Just be sure you show it—don't hide your light under a basket.

anaclisis *n.* fancy psychological term for why you date women who wear shoes like your Aunt Betsy's.

angelology *n.* the study of all things angelic, beginning with the physical beauty of women. Many see no need to study further.

angry *adj.* something a guy has to get, once in a while, publicly, to avoid being dismissed as a "nice guy."

angst *n.* a fancy word for "nervousness."

anniversary *n.* a burden to remember, a horror to forget.

apologize *v.* to cut an argument short.

arousal *n.* sexual or emotional stimulation. While men hate arousal without consummation, women hate consummation without arousal.

ask *v.* to indicate that you are not paying attention and need a concept explained again. *To ask for*—to wonder aloud about an item until it is given to you as a gift.

assault rifle *n.* a gun for human beings designed by a man who decided killing animals was fun but insufficient. (The bulletproof vest was invented by a woman.)

assertive *adj.* free of self-doubt and therefore able to instill it in others.

arousal *n.* an awareness of anger, lust, fear, or lust.

ask *v.* to sacrifice power. To lay in the muck and grovel.

assault rifle *n.* complement to a pepper rifle, this essential weapon helps a man protect his family from hordes of marauding deer.

assertive *adj.* what a woman is being when—shaking and, in some states, cursing—she finally tells you what she wants. You are expected to congratulate her honesty and satisfy the demand.

B

babe *n*. an insulting nickname unless used by Lou Reed.

baby *n*. an infant; the only one in the family who really appreciates baby talk.

back *n*. a body part that is turned toward you when those nearby feel the need to be hostile or to be massaged.

baggage *n*. stuff people carry into airplanes and marriages, despite all attempts to get them to check it in.

bald *adj*. lacking hair or disguise. *When Lloyd told Jan he had a business meeting at 10 P.M., she sensed it was a bald lie.*

ballroom dancing *n*. an activity in which women can find Old-World gentility, etiquette, adoration, and flattery—without the political oppression that originally came with those things.

bar *n*. a place where you can meet people who appear to have no idea of their level of attractiveness and may or may not be alcoholics.

basic *adj*. **1.** essential. **2.** a shade of black.

beard *n*. **1.** a fashion choice that Santa, Abraham Lincoln, and a handful of other men can pull off with success. The rest should not even try. **2.** an early twentieth-century term for "third wheel."

beau *n*. a boyfriend who knows how to waltz.

B

babe *n*. a compliment that is rarely taken as one. Go figure.

baby *n*. larval stage of the common adolescent.

back *n*. the part of a woman's body that neither looks at you nor talks to you. Often lovely.

baggage *n. pl.* heavy objects you're expected to carry when traveling with a woman. So it is wise to pack lightly for yourself.

bald *adj*. open and vulnerable. *Lloyd was feeling particularly bald that night, as he held Anne.*

ballroom dancing *n*. a decent skill to have. You don't want to be like Abe Lincoln, who approached Mary Todd with the line, "Miss Todd, I want to dance with you in the worst way." Mary said later, "And that's just what he did." Lincoln was so embarrassed, he married her.

bar *n*. a place a man goes to stare at distant women and talk to the ones God brings close. While waiting for God to bring more, he can talk about football, and get drunk.

basic *adj*. a thing that should be obvious. *"Steve," the bartender shouted, "roses for Valentine's Day is just basic!"*

beard *n*. **1.** something to grow as soon as you can, if people aren't giving you respect. **2.** Chaucer's euphemism, pirated by male high school students ever since, for a woman's pubic hair.

beau *n*. French word meaning "rich boyfriend."

beautiful 1. *adj.* stirring, lovely. *What a beautiful sentiment.* **2.** A fine compliment, especially effective in noun form. *"Hi, beautiful"* is guaranteed to topple the most self-assured woman. There <u>is</u> no response. What's she supposed to answer? *"Hello, earthling"?*

beauty *n.* **1.** pain. **2.** a serene aesthetic quality. **3.** A goal to achieve, often associated with hot rollers and pain.

bediquette *n.* polite conduct for bedroom guests. Includes remembering guests' names and repeating them occasionally, asking guests if they had a good time, and saying you had one.

best friend *n.* an individual you telephone daily.

better *adj.* what women have to be in order to be considered remotely good.

big *adj.* a word men need to hear constantly.

bimbo *n.* a woman who successfully wears lycra thongs in public.

bitch *n.* a woman who realizes that being nice only gets you halfway to your destination.

blind date *n.* **1.** a last resort. **2.** a disaster accompanied by a free meal. **3.** a fine way to lose a close friend. *Ellen fixed Melinda up on a blind date, and they haven't spoken since.*

blocks *n. pl.* **1.** emotional obstacles. *Melinda stopped dating Mitch when she realized how many blocks he had.* **2.** toys. *Mitch would probably enjoy playing with blocks.*

beautiful *adj.* an event or object exalted above the normal range. Carlton Fisk's home run in the sixth game of the 1975 World Series remains beautiful—it did not even need to be followed by a win in the seventh game. Which was just as well.

beauty *n.* **1.** anything pleasing to the senses. Physical beauty is only skin-deep—but that can be plenty.

bediquette *n.* manners made crucial by the greater exposure of guests' nerves. It is impolite to laugh at another's endowment. Or to clear one's throat and spit.

best friend *n.* the one you call a few days after breaking up with a woman you love, or as soon as you can keep your voice steady.

better *adj.* a word describing improved quality but often seen in terms of quantity. This stereo is better for your bedroom because it puts out more decibels; that girlfriend is better, for the same reason.

big *adj.* what your muscles ought to be, if your Mr. Happy isn't.

bimbo *n.* a friendly, attractive woman who will not criticize your grammar, even if you end a sentence with a proposition.

bitch *n.* a woman who doesn't realize that women are supposed to be nicer than men.

blind date *n.* an encounter from which you may find yourself glad you can see to drive home.

blocks *n. pl.* **1.** hard objects on which to put your car to rest, during winter. **2.** hard methods by which to put your opponents to rest, during football.

blood *n.* a source of life; a symbol of death; a destroyer of perfectly good underwear.

blue balls *n. pl.* discomfort men feel when their passion is not consummated. Women just get the blues.

blush *n.* **1.** a powdery makeup that pinkens the face. **2.** the color of rosé wine that can also pinken the face.

boast *v.* to speak so highly of yourself that you alienate those around you.

boredom *n.* when you don't have anything to dote on.

boyfriend *n.* someone who calls at least every other day and who is available Saturday night. Like a pet, a boyfriend is an all-purpose companion. Though harder to train.

bra *n.* an article of clothing that you long to wear when you don't need it and long to take off when you do.

braggadocio *n.* how overconfident people refer to their meager talent.

breaking up *n.* an unpleasant process during which you destroy someone's ego to preserve your own and anything you say may be used against you later, ensuring a permanent separation from a person you adore. Especially painful if the other person snuggles really well.

blood *n.* evidence of a wound, generally. Women are said to be squeamish about blood that comes from a wound; men, about blood that does <u>not</u> come from a wound.

blue balls *n. pl.* a condition of sexual frustration in which the excited male gonads ache because they cannot burst. Guilt-tripping boyfriends notwithstanding, most men old enough to reach this state can relieve it without help.

blush *v.* to turn red, at the exact moment you least want to turn red. Mark Twain: *"Man is the only animal that blushes. Or needs to."*

boast *v.* to speak so highly of yourself that you intimidate those around you.

boredom *n.* when you can't go to bed with anyone new.

boyfriend *n.* a title allowing you the exclusive lease on a specified woman, for an unspecified period of time, including an option to buy. Conditions may vary. See previous lessee for details.

bra *n.* a protective device that is harder to remove than its counterpart to the south.

braggadocio *n.* how jealous people refer to your self-assessment.

breaking up *n.* thanks to fax machines, no longer as hard to do.

breasts *n. pl.* sensitive fixtures used to enhance clothing, impede running, and nurse infants. May serve as social indicators: one can point them in the direction of the person one would like to be talking to, even if one is talking to someone else. This is known as "body language." There are people who only seem able to make eye contact with breasts. They are known as "bad dinner companions."

bride *n.* a woman about to get married who traditionally wears such extraordinary outfits that she becomes the center of nonstop attention for several days running. This is to compensate for the fact that other men will soon pay her less attention.

bridesmaid *n.* what you turn into when someone you thought was your best friend gets married and appoints you one of a bevy of personal slaves in hideous identical dresses.

brother *n.* **1.** someone to use as target practice. **2.** a source of information about boys. **3.** a receptacle of information about girls.

bull *n.* **1.** apocryphal stories that are designed to impress. **2.** an animal whose well-attended slaughter is designed to impress.

bump *v.* **1.** *bump off:* to murder, with purpose. **2.** *bump into:* to meet, by accident. **3.** *bump and grind:* to twist one's pelvis, on the dance floor, with purpose.

burp *v.* to make a sound after eating. While some cultures consider it rude, other cultures consider it a sign of appreciation for a good meal. Male culture is one of these.

busy *adj.* utterly swamped unless someone special calls.

butch *adj.* what a woman with traditionally masculine qualities is called. A man with traditionally feminine qualities is called "sensitive."

breasts *n. pl.* female appendages, to which infants look for milk. Many of us didn't get enough, so we keep looking.

bride *n.* what you end up with when your emotions get the best of you.

bridesmaid *n.* someone to hit on at a wedding: she's usually vulnerable.

brother *n.* the guy you could have been, if your sperm had missed your egg. Some love these modified versions of themselves. Others, like Cain, are less thrilled.

bull *n.* **1.** a strong, silent male. **2.** a disingenuous tale.

bump *n.* **1.** one of the things not to call a breast. **2.** a meaningless obstacle. A word that helps reframe the issue, if you are caught cheating. *"Honey, this is just a bump on our relationship highway."*

burp *v.* to release gas via the mouth, resulting in a feeling of relief. Some people do this aloud, to share their joy.

busy *adj.* utterly swamped unless someone special dies.

butch *adj.* a short haircut.

C

call *n.* a phone call; an intimation of caring; an admission of need; a subtle proclamation of desire or friendship.

car *n.* **1.** a thing that goes *vroom*; a way of getting places. **2.** an item women notice if it belongs to us. Men notice other people's cars, and will say, "That's the same green Chevy that was tailing us two hours ago." They are not paranoid, just car-conscious.

career *n.* an arena for fulfilling potential, helping others, and being judged constantly. *Melinda wondered if her new hairstyle would hurt her career.*

change *v.* **1.** to improve, develop, mature. *Lloyd has a few faults, but he will change.* **2.** to dress in a more appropriate set of clothes. *If we go directly from the Plaza to the Nasti Klub, I'm going to have to change.*

channel-surf *v.* to watch segments of TV shows in an attempt to learn all there is to know and then decide what to watch. Men may change channels in the middle of a sentence as if they aren't the least bit curious as to how it ends. *Lloyd switched channels right after the cop on the dramedy said there was one method of revenge that always worked, and Jan never got to find out what it was.*

charity *n.* a place to give your time when you don't have enough money.

charm *v.* to behave so adorably that it seems there's nothing wrong with you.

chaste *adj.* a state of sexual inactivity and purity. Women used to wear special belts to prove that they were chaste. Now they just wear special frowns.

C

call *v.* what you should do a few days after fooling around, if you want to do it again.

car *n.* something a guy is expected to know about. A no-win: if he knows and cares a lot about cars, she'll tease him; if the car breaks and he knows nothing, she'll curse him.

career *n.* fancy word for "job." *Steve wondered if "eternal student" counted as a career.*

change *v.* something he's expected to do, for her. Something she's already done, for him. (Don't question her on this—it'll get worse.)

channel-surf *v.* to zap between stations. You surf because you can. You surf because no single channel owns you, but you can ride them all. *Lloyd wished he could channel-surf between Jan and Anne as easily as between Leno and Letterman.*

charity *n.* a place to give your money when you don't have enough time.

charm *n.* beauty. *On Letterman, Cindy Crawford, full of charm, said almost nothing.*

chaste *adj.* virginal. At first she won't enjoy having sex with you. Then she'll wonder: Could it be even better, with someone else?

cheat *v.* to behave dishonestly in order to pass a test or leave a relationship.

cheerleader *n.* a girl who can win a football game using only a few gymnastics, a little skirt, and a big mouth.

child *n.* something to be for as long as possible, and then to think about having.

children *n. pl.* people to be nurtured, idealized, and loved. Includes offspring and men.

chocolate *n.* an essential food with consoling powers. Happily, causes the brain to secrete serotonin—the same chemical it secretes after sex, but without all the bother.

Cinderella *n.* the woman who started the myth that if you sweep enough floors without complaining, an incredible man will notice you, take you to a big party, and humiliate your most hated relatives.

circumcision *n.* like ear-piercing, an accepted and encouraged form of minor mutilation best gotten over with early in life.

circumvent *v.* to avoid by taking a different route. To see how two completely unrelated subjects are intimately related, especially when you would like to bypass one of them in conversation.

cheat *v.* to behave dishonestly in order to pass a test or maintain a relationship.

cheerleader *n.* a pert, healthy young woman who encourages young men to maim each other.

child *n.* **1.** any woman under sixteen. Unwise to date them, unless you are that age, too. And mostly even then. **2.** something a woman remembers to want before a man does. *"Everything about woman is a riddle, and everything about woman has one solution: pregnancy."*—Friedrich Nietzsche.

children *n. pl.* small versions of adults, with bigger needs. Sometimes, when these come along, a guy will see life in a whole new way. He'll see that he is no longer needed, except to pay the bills.

chocolate *n.* substance to offer a woman, to get her in the mood.

Cinderella *n.* the woman who started the myth that if you marry well, you can skip a few rungs on that pesky corporate ladder. She is the archetype for romance novels, and for the otherwise masculine Boston Red Sox, whose coach never fails to become a pumpkin by October.

circumcision *n.* painful removal of the foreskin, which may eventually dull the remaining nerves, and so reduce erotic sensation. Which might be just as well— we get enough complaints as it is.

circumvent *v.* to go around. What a wily man does to a woman's sexual defenses, when he is not sufficiently famous for a direct approach. *With poems and chocolate and condoms, Tony was ready to circumvent every obstacle. Now all he needed was a date.*

clam 1. *n.* an introverted mollusk. **2.** *v. to clam up:* to become exasperatingly quiet; to refuse to discuss the matter at hand; to behave like an introverted mollusk.

clandestine *adj.* secretive. *Clandestine affair:* a relationship that can exasperate its participants, turning undemonstrative people into hand-holding nitwits. May cause depression, coldness, and statements like, "My feelings are too advanced for me to be satisfied by my unofficial status." This is logical and thus not good, because logic will kill the clandestine affair.

clean *v.* to render pristine. There are several options: find a finicky spouse, find affordable household help (which may hurt your chances of being elected to Congress), or do it yourself.

clear *adj.* easy to understand, sometimes so easy to understand that the magic dies. *It was clear from his lusty wink that Al wanted Anne.*

cleavage *n.* a shadowy mirage that can form between breasts. Has a life of its own. Clothes that intensify this phenomenon should be worn sparingly and in desperate situations.

climax *n.* **1.** the point in a film when you dig your nails into his arm. **2.** the point in bed when you dig your nails into his back.

clinch *v.* to close a deal or confirm an opinion. *Melinda had already pretty much decided not to date Parker, but when she saw his zebra rug, that clinched it.*

clam *n.* **1.** an uncommunicative man. **2.** an obscene, gross, vile designation, which we would never repeat, for female genitalia.

clandestine *adj.* concealed, as would be a trip to a psychiatrist or a mistress. To say nothing of a psychiatrist's mistress.

clean *adj.* describing any room you can walk through.

clear *adj.* the opposite of vague. When you feel inarticulate, it's best to imply that you *are* being clear, it's just that your conversational partner has the comprehension level of a moth. *Lloyd wondered if he should get up and talk to Al and make everything perfectly clear. Trouble was, it wasn't clear to Lloyd.*

cleavage *n.* the space between a woman's breasts, often including a glimpse of the breasts themselves. A fine place to sleep.

climax *n.* explosion signifying the end of a movie or date. A fine time to sleep.

clinch *n.* an effective wrestling move. *Parker had used the rug often, to practice his Iowa clinch.*

cling v. **1.** to glue oneself to a specific idea, plan, or guy. Not a good idea if you really want to hang on to any of them. **2.** to adhere snugly, as in clothing. *Melinda refused to buy a skirt that didn't cling to her thighs.* **3.** *n. static cling:* a state of aesthetic disaster caused by invisible but nasty electric particles.

close *adj.* in the same emotional precinct.

close-mouthed *adj.* speaking-impaired.

closet *n.* a place to store clothing, old skis, and latent sexualities. If you have a lot of such things, you may need a walk-in closet.

clothes *n. pl.* the windows of the soul.

coaching *n.* special prompting, required by the unathletic and the dense.

codependency *n.* when you find yourself bribing casino dealers so your honey will win one round of blackjack and take you home.

coffee *n.* brewed caffeine. Kills the appetite. Due to the dieting craze, a popular drink for women. Like a bad lover, coffee makes your heart race, makes you nervous and jittery, and makes you feel you can't function without it. Any wonder we go back for more?

cognac *n.* **1.** a cake ingredient. **2.** a beverage drunk out of sexy brandy glasses.

cohabit *v.* to sacrifice some closet space in order to have him around. A trade-off.

cling *v.* to preserve old baseball cards, yearbooks, and photos of ex-girlfriends.

close *v.* to shut tight, as an inner door on an emotion.

close-mouthed *adj.* reticent. Don't confuse it with close-minded.

closet *n.* a place to hang jackets and store boxes containing favored issues of *Playboy* or other things you're not ready to lose or share.

clothes *n. pl.* the doors of the body.

coaching *n.* physical teaching, ignored by the omniscient and the foolish.

codependency *n.* **1.** a term women use when they don't want to be emotionally supportive. *"I don't want to be codependent, Lloyd," said Jan, "so I'm going to the movies with Phoebe."* **2.** a term men can use when they don't want to be financially supportive. *"I don't want to be codependent, Jan," said Lloyd, "so I'm taking the life insurance money to Vegas."*

coffee *n.* a beverage that increases inhibitions and keeps you alert. Good for a blind date.

cognac *n.* expensive but, according to a Russian source, makes up for the price by increasing your potency.

cohabit *v.* to obtain exclusive milking rights, with an option to buy the cow.

collude *v.* to act in concert, secretly. Something a man and a woman do, at times, to pretend their relationship is better than it is.

cologne *n.* perfumed toilet water that is cheaper than perfume and pricier than toilet water. Can enhance the attractiveness of both men and women, as long as couples don't have a basic cologne conflict.

come *v.* to arrive, and to realize there's no going back.

comfort *n.* when you can kick off your shoes; when no one is criticizing you; when you can indulge in as much ice cream as you want.

commit *v.* to pay unwarranted attention to someone in case they suddenly become worthy of that attention.

commitment *n.* when you know his shirt size. *See* RELATIONSHIP.

commitmentphobic *adj.* seductive and princely, and then suddenly, inexplicably claustrophic toward loved ones. Incapable of making concrete plans.

compassion *n.* generosity of spirit summoned for those you love, those you understand, and those who are completely pathetic. *Melinda had compassion for Parker.*

competition *n.* behavior that occurs when a man is physically incapable of enjoying a woman's success, or when "confident" people feel the need to prove their superiority.

complain *v.* the cathartic process of announcing your problems to anyone who will listen. *Melinda complained to Hank that she hated her job. When he suggested she quit, she said no, she loved her job, she just hated it this week and wanted to complain.*

collude *v.* to act in concert, secretly. Something a man and a woman do, at times, to pretend their relationship is better than it is.

cologne *n.* a scented liquid not intended for use as a deodorant.

come *v.* an action a man may labor hours to induce in a woman, which she may coax from him in minutes, by lying still.

comfort *n.* a feeling of security women offer with their eyes and their words, and men offer with their size and their wallets.

commit *v.* to confine a person for a specified period of time, as to a mental institution.

commitment *n.* a way to say "we might get married" without actually saying it.

commitmentphobic *adj.* a term invented to patholo-gize a healthy fear.

compassion *n.* being nice to a person whose loss is not your own, as to a young woman whose boyfriend has moved away.

competition *n.* behavior that occurs because access to females is limited and life is short.

complain *v.* to kvetch. Because older men teach younger men not to complain, the refrain "Men are no damn good" has gone largely unanswered.

complex 1. *adj.* complicated. **2.** *n.* a personal neurosis. Common ones include the Oedipus Complex, in which the son is attracted to the mother; the Electra Complex, in which the daughter is attracted to the father; and the Inferiority Complex, in which the child is attracted to anyone who will speak to him.

computer *n.* an entity that does household tasks without arguing and doesn't mind just being friends. *Melinda named her new computer Max.*

conception *n.* the sunny realization that something is growing inside you. Like stomach butterflies and heart twitters, but better.

condom *n.* an essential household item; the Tupperware of postmodernism.

confidence *n.* complete faith in oneself. Nourished by hard work, encouragement, compliments, and a steadily growing set of breasts.

confront *v.* to tell the naked truth and have everyone yell at you. *Jan thought the waiter had short-changed her by a dollar, but didn't want to confront him because he might get mad.*

conquest *n.* a siege in war or love in which defenses are gradually worn down. The more obstacles to overcome, the more interesting for the conqueror.

consent *v.* to state officially you will allow that which anyone with half a brain can see you will allow.

control *n.* power over the course of things, enjoyed most by those who believe that emotions can get in the way of a really good relationship.

conversation *n.* the secret to meaningful interaction, meaningful sex, and meaning.

complex *n.* **1**. a sports arena, with room for baseball and basketball. **2**. a neurosis, with room for boasting and insecurity.

computer *n.* a machine that goes the phone one better: now you can converse, not only without smelling or seeing other people, but also without hearing them.

conception *n.* an idea (usually a bad one).

condom *n.* an item of clothing, as important today as the necktie once was. And with a similar choking effect.

confidence *n.* the aura of pride you need if you want to have sex, which you may obtain only by having sex.

confront *v.* to tell someone he's been caught. *Lloyd adored women who couldn't confront him.*

conquest *n.* a victory. It is inevitable to feel this the first time a woman shares her body. The feeling should ebb, as it becomes increasingly clear that she wanted you to do what you did. If that does not become clear, you may have committed a crime. Check local statutes.

consent *n.* a green light. Not "a red light that *wanted* to be green."

control *n.* like "cognito," a place you most want to be "in" when everything goes to hell.

conversation *n.* foreplay.

convert *n.* someone who comes around to your way of seeing things.

conviction *n.* a belief so powerful that it can help you endure or ignore almost anything.

cooking *n.* **1.** a mode of expressing lasting affection. **2.** an activity in which one exaggerates one's interest and experience; especially popular during courtship.

coward *n.* **1.** a person incapable of doing the right thing, such as men who skip battles or child-support payments. **2.** what a man calls you when you decline to cross the street against the light at a crowded intersection.

creativity *n.* the ability to imagine that makes for good art and great lying. *Lloyd explained Anne's visit to Jan with tremendous creativity.*

crime *n.* not our scene. Too messy and gory. Why stage a robbery, when it's easier just to put it on the credit card and not be able to pay the bill?

cruelty *n.* inexcusably mean behavior. Can involve touching, refusing to touch, lying, telling the truth, yelling, or silence.

crush *n.* a queasy feeling that all will not be right with the world until a certain man announces his intentions to have his way with you.

cry *v.* what women do instead of punching the wall. (Men punch the wall because they are not supposed to cry and it pisses them off.)

convert *v.* to adopt a new belief, as a result of logical persuasion, threats or bribes. *Lloyd knew Anne didn't want to be his "other woman," but he hoped a nice necklace would convert her.*

conviction *n.* a belief that bores or threatens everyone but its holder.

cooking *n.* the heating and moistening of spaghetti. Makes a great date—it's cheaper than going out, she'll think you "sensitive," and best of all, she's already at your place.

coward *n.* **1.** a word a man may spend his whole life avoiding, by killing anything that makes him feel he might be one. **2.** what a woman calls you when you decline to rush headlong into an emotionally violent argument.

creativity *n.* the ability to draw on the past, but produce something new. Pitching to Reggie Jackson required this, as does guarding Jerry Rice. Sportscasters don't need as much creativity, as long as they know phrases like "That's *gotta* hurt."

crime *n.* a well-traveled route to a woman's heart, if you can't do the college thing. And even if you can. Makes them want to tame you.

cruelty *n.* whatever made her cry <u>this</u> time.

crush *v.* to reduce a beer can in one's palm to one-tenth original size.

cry *v.* something men are allowed to do at movies, and women whenever they like. Prevents ulcers.

cute *adj.* **1.** a word men hate to hear used applied to themselves because they think it diminishes them. **2.** good-looking or charming; heaven-sent. **3.** appealing due to romantic goopiness. *What a cute restaurant.* **4.** appealing due to extra-long eyelashes. *What a cute puppy.* **5.** appealing due to good interior decorating. *What cute doorknobs.*

cyberflirt *n.* someone who sees the Internet as a singles bar. *Melinda, tired of avoiding calls from the other losers she was dating, signed on to the 'Net (screen-name: Melinda5) and met gradstud, a cyberflirt. She asked him what he was studying.*

cynical *adj.* romance-hating.

cute *adj*. a word applied to friendly, attractive women and to unthreatening boys.

cyberflirt *n*. a person who's gifted with her hands and knows how to look good onscreen. *After talking to Melinda5, Steve signed on again and met a cyberflirt named Bubbles, who asked him how much of a stud he was and how he intended to prove it.*

cynical *adj*. what you will be accused of being if you notice, aloud, that women who complain about jerks rarely leave them.

D

DIALECTS OF THE MALE AND FEMALE LANGUAGES

Male and Female dialects flourished at the beginning of the twentieth century, starting with the development of Macho Dialect. At first, Macho Dialect consisted of words and phrases meaning "woman"—*chick, babe, babydoll, doll, dollface, broad, dame* (archaic), *moll* (archaic). Loose variants were *floozy* and *bimbo*. The words meant any woman at all, then began to mean "a desirable woman," and then, due to changing attitudes, "a desirable woman who doesn't like this term, so I am using it behind her back."

Women, disgusted at being talked about behind their backs, invented Anti-Macho Dialect to keep men in their place: a series of words meaning "a man" or "a guy who doesn't get it": *pig, twerp, creep, dolt, dork, twit, lunk, jerk, dweeb, numbnuts, sleazebag, dingbat, pondscum*.

But these words weren't enough for early feminists, who found Macho Dialect degrading and fought to eliminate it. Men were confused because they intended their dialect to be flattering, but soon changed their ways.

D

dance *n.* a conversation in body language that may or may not lead anywhere. The ultimate safe sex, since you can always say, "I thought this was just a dance."

darling 1. *adj.* slightly archaic. Sweet, poignant. *"What a darling dress."* **2.** *n.* a term of endearment often combined with a compliment or an insult, as in *"Darling, you're a genius,"* or *"Darling, you're an idiot."*

Macho Dialect was driven underground. Soon the only men you could find saying "doll" or "dame" or "babe" were Humphrey Bogart and Clark Gable. Like back-seamed pantyhose, the words were destined to return, this time with humor.

Then Lou Reed wrote the lyrics, "Hey, Babe, take a walk on the Wild Side," calling into question the idea that the word "babe" had ever been an insult.

Post-feminists argued that rather than abolish the objectification of women, women should simply objectify men equally. They felt men would eventually be forced to shave their legs and wear uncomfortable undergarments. With this goal in mind, Post-Feminist Dialect came into being, offering a series of words for "good-looking and slow-thinking man": *himbo, bimboy, hunkola, beef-cake, studmuffin.*

So it is that regional dialects reflect gender upheavals. Now women playfully use Macho Dialect, calling each other "babe" when necessary, and men have been heard affectionately addressing each other in Anti-Macho Dialect— "Hey, numbnuts!" a man might say to a dear friend.

And stupidity is now reaching the threshold of equality. The female "ditz" and the male "dimwit" are commonly replaced by the useful gender-neutral expression: "Pretty house, but no one's home."

—*JLB*

D

dance *n.* a socially acceptable way to get a woman's attention, without having to talk.

darling *n.* term of endearment, to be used liberally only if you are wealthy or Southern.

date 1. *n.* a couple's planned wedding day. *Do you have a date?* **2.** *v.* to endure countless morons in the hopes of meeting one normal person.

date rape *n.* when your rapist takes you to dinner first.

dating *v.* the process of receiving constant serenades, love notes, and brief poems on the nature of passion.

dating around *v.* a way to keep a roster of male suitors in gridlock.

daughter *n.* someone to whom you impart notions of womanhood and hope she is too busy rebelling against you to make any of the same mistakes you did.

dead *adj.* **1.** no longer living. **2.** so deep in the proverbial doghouse that you might as well be no longer living.

dear *adj., n.* a term of endearment: useful for starting letters or eluding criticism. *"Yes, dear, whatever you say, dear."*

death *n.* the end of life, hopefully with more to come.

debauchery *n.* partying without limitations. *Bubbles was riveted when Steve asked her if it was possible to simulate debauchery on the Internet.*

debutante *n.* a girl with a pastel dress and a pastel personality who somehow gets the best dates.

deceive *v.* to neglect to correct a misapprehension.

definite *adj.* absolutely certain. Men enjoy pretending to be definite. We would rather waste time pretending to be perfect.

degeneration *n.* when the prince turns back into a frog.

date *n.* a socially acceptable way to get a woman alone.

date rape *n.* to be avoided. One more night of masturbation at home beats (so to speak) a thousand such nights in prison.

dating *v.* **1.** sleeping together. **2.** what she calls your "relationship," if you're not "committed."

dating around *v.* a way to get two or three women alone.

daughter *n.* female child, through whom a man may finally see true femininity, unsullied by his desires.

dead *adj.* the football after a whistle has blown, or your enemy after an artery has blown. After a brief pause, play may resume.

dear *n.* all-purpose shorthand, if you have forgotten a woman's name.

death *n.* the end of someone else's life.

debauchery *n.* mutually assured dissipation. *"A little debauchery can be good for the soul,"* Steve wrote to Bubbles, *"as long as you stop at 'a little.'"*

debutante *n.* a woman so valuable her puberty is cause for a party.

deceive *v.* to feign love when one feels only lust. Works best when one is oneself deceived.

definite *adj.* the opposite of annoying.

degeneration *n.* when the princess turns into a crone.

demonstrate *v.* to convince by exemplary behavior. Much more effective than convincing by a long speech, since long speeches are boring. *Melinda had tired of men who talked about love without demonstrating that they loved her.*

denouement *n.* the final phase of an event, when it peters out, lingers, and thankfully dies.

depressed *adj.* when you feel the world might end, it would be good if it did, and it would be your fault. A contagious state.

description *n.* a crucial part of a story, occasionally interrupted by action. A good description of his facial expression when it happened beats anything that might have happened.

desire *n.* emotionally charged lust.

detachment *n.* the act of cutting oneself off emotionally at the first sign of pain, because one does not yet realize that feeling bad is better than not feeling at all.

diamond *n.* the most indestructible gem, and a symbol of lasting relationships. Constructed of complex carbons and feelings. Diamonds are often understood to be a girl's best friend. While this is absurd, they're not her worst enemy, either.

diet *n.* an ancient form of self-torture involving numerous cantaloupes.

different *adj.* the same. *When Phoebe told the womanizer she didn't want to be womanized, he assured her, "This is different."*

dim *adj.* describes a sort of people and lighting that flatter you but then leave you with a headache.

direct *adj.* outright, explicit, dull.

demonstrate *v.* to show, as by explicating a mathematical proof, marching in protest, or doffing one's clothes.

denouement *n.* the stuff that happens after the climax of a movie or date. Can usually be slept through safely.

depressed *adj.* when you can see life as it is. Treatable with drugs, exercise, and positive thinking (a.k.a. "denial").

description *n.* the part of the book where the author entertains himself more than his reader. The more time a book spends on description, the less time there is for anything to happen.

desire *n.* lust.

detachment *n.* the ability to keep one's emotions at bay. Coolness.

diamond *n.* a rock for which you go into hock.

diet *n.* a plan to cut back on Doritos with your beer.

different *adj.* not identical. *When Phoebe asked why it was different, the womanizer said, "Because you, my dear, are so different." She bought it.*

dim *adj.* dull. *One of Dan Quayle's former professors at DePauw described the former vice-president as "a dim bulb."*

direct *v.* to control.

discipline *n.* inner strength and will. Essential for dieting, tai chi, attending military academies, and suing military academies in order to attend them.

dishonesty *n.* the telling of partial truths in order to avoid hurting others.

disillusionment *n.* the stepping-stone to maturity; the evaporation of trusty clichés and classic hopes into little piles of dust.

distance *n.* the invisible barrier between people who would otherwise be great friends or decent spouses.

distant *adj.* **1.** in another country or state. **2.** in another emotional country or state.

divert *v.* **1.** to distract by entertaining. **2.** to shift attention or funding to the place it is most needed.

divorce 1. *v.* to fail as a marriage. **2.** *n.* a painful process through which one becomes a divorcée —a wise, oversexed person.

dizzy *adj.* given to falling over. Can be a symptom of any of a number of trendy dilemmas: eating disorders, Chronic Fatigue Syndrome, obsessive love. *See* FAINT.

doll *n.* a perfect human being; a docile toy. While boys do have dolls, they are always male; girls play with both male and female dolls. This explains a lot.

domination *n.* when you choose to tickle instead of being tickled.

dream *n.* the truth that you know—and the rest of the world has yet to discover.

discipline *n.* the ability to ignore distractions and press on. Easier to achieve if your mind is limited and you don't notice the distractions in the first place.

dishonesty *n.* lying.

disillusionment *n.* the loss of a pleasant dishonesty—makeup, for example.

distance *n.* space. You need distance most from those who give you the least.

distant *adj.* how a woman may describe you, if you don't quit your job to listen to her.

divert *v.* to deflect. What a man tries to do, to the admiring glance a stranger aims at "his" woman (by moving closer to her, brushing his fingers on her arm, and glaring at the starer), while simultaneously diverting the attention of "his" woman away from that man, ideally before she notices the stare.

divorce *v.* to dissolve, as a marriage. A word savored only by your lawyer and your mistress.

dizzy *adj.* how you feel the first time an attractive woman smiles on you—and each time thereafter.

doll *n.* something respectable men used to call women. It was a compliment.

domination *n.* when no one dares tickle you.

dream *n.* the desire that you know—and hope the rest of the world will never discover.

dress *v.* to throw clothes on the floor, while dabbing nail polish on the run in your nylons and realizing that none of your shoes matches anything else you own.

drive 1. *n.* ambition. *He liked her drive.* **2.** *v.* to navigate a car. *He liked her to drive.*

drone 1. *v.* to go on and on. **2.** *n.* a bee who serves the queen. (Females do dominate the insect world, whatever that's worth.)

drugs *n. pl.* **1.** items promoted and sold mostly by men before they go into politics and fight against them. **2.** medications prescribed to fight infections, depression, and boredom.

drunk *adj.* a state in which you do things you later regret.

Dutch *adj.* the practice of splitting the tab on unsuccessful dates. If he likes you he should pay to prove chivalry is not dead, and if you like him you should pay so he'll feel guilty and take you out again. If you don't like each other, go Dutch.

dress *v.* to wear what is reasonably clean.

drive 1. *v.* to hit powerfully, as a golf ball or a baseball. 2. *n.* a passion for something, as for success, food, or whoopee. 3. *v.* to maneuver, as a car or other vehicle. *"Bend over, honey—I'll drive."*

drone *n.* a man who doesn't work, has no sting, and makes no honey.

drugs *n. pl.* substances that fiddle with your brain, sometimes successfully.

drunk *adj.* a state in which you do things you later forget.

Dutch *adj.* a treat for your wallet, but maybe less so for the organ next to your wallet.

E

eager *adj.* **1.** impatient to love. **2.** overly excited. **3.** how puppies and boys are. More endearing in puppies.

early *adj.* prompt. There are early people and late people. Many women start life as early people, then discover that no one is there to meet them and become late people—or just bitter.

earnest *adj.* so honest that you volunteer self-undermining information.

earring *n.* jewelry that reveals character. Two earrings say she has a basic threshold for pain, three signify adventurousness, and four indicate she lacks judgment in her analysis of trends.

earth mother *n.* a woman who nurtures passersby, produces children effortlessly, and wears funky shoes.

easy *adj.* **1.** laid-back, relaxed. *"Don't worry, I'm easy."* **2.** sexually laid-back, relaxed. *"Don't worry, she's easy."*

eat *v.* to have a sexual experience without needing to call your lover.

eavesdrop *v.* to participate vicariously in a conversation simply by overhearing it.

effort *n.* collective or individual will. *A group effort.* Sadly, effort can lead nowhere. *Jan had her colors done in an effort to put some life back into her dying marriage. She discovered she was a winter.*

egocentric *adj.* utterly self-centered. A sign that someone is either a complete jerk or has been in psychoanalysis for too long.

E

eager *adj.* to be excited about something that may not happen. One of the first feelings a man learns to hide—because showing eagerness can *ensure* the thing won't happen.

early *adj.* what you ought not be for a date, so as not to appear too eager.

earnest *adj.* humorless. An appropriate trait, for occupations like "banker."

earring *n.* an ornament on which it's good to nibble.

earth mother *n.* a woman who doesn't wear miniskirts or shave her armpits.

easy *adj.* the type of woman you don't bring home to mother, because there just isn't time.

eat *v.* **1.** to engulf, chewing as necessary. **2.** to give an oral performance that requires few encouraging words—although "thank you" comes to mind.

eavesdrop *v.* to passively pry. Men frown on this, since eavesdropping does not allow us to interrupt.

effort *n.* something that makes you sweat.

egocentric *adj.* anyone who can't see that the world doesn't revolve around him but instead revolves around me.

egomania *n.* a condition in which the afflicted takes the question "How are you?" literally.

egregious *adj.* embarrassingly bad. *Jan's color consultant told her that since she was a winter, it would be an egregious error for her to wear yellow.*

elegant *adj.* embodying the art of dressing divinely and not talking too much.

eligible *adj.* describes a bachelor who does dashing things while remaining emotionally stable.

eloquence *n.* the ability to convince anyone of anything whether you believe it or not.

embarrass *v.* to mortify. Easy to do to teenagers. Also to men, except men will be embarrassed that they were embarrassed and may not be able to talk to you again.

emoticon *n.* sideways smiley faces that indicate tone on the Internet. *Bubbles told Steve he was no good at cybersex, and followed the statement with the happy emoticon :-) so he could tell she was just kidding.*

empathy *n.* walking in the shoes of others, feeling all their problems as keenly as if they were yours. A female specialty. Our own problems just aren't enough for us.

empire 1. *n.* an extensive kingdom with lots of zip codes and subjugation. **2.** *adj.* refers to a vague waistline popular in the reign of the Empress Josephine, now particularly useful for pregnant brides.

employee *n.* someone who gets blamed for your worst mistakes.

egomania *n.* a disease you detect in the person who dumps you.

egregious *adj.* a major error, such as forgetting to tag at third on a deep fly ball.

elegant *adj.* when you wear dark socks with shoes. With shorts, you don't need the socks.

eligible *adj.* describes a woman who flirts.

eloquence *n.* the ability to make gray areas look silver.

embarrass *v.* to cause to blush and/or giggle. Easy to do to women: talk about another woman exactly the way you would describe her to men. (A woman who does not become embarrassed is one with whom you may be honest.)

emoticon *n.* a method of expressing emotion without moving a facial muscle or saying word one. *Steve had never seen an emoticon, didn't understand it, and felt insulted.*

empathy *n.* acknowledging another's pain. *Steve, looking for empathy, explained to Tim how insulted he had felt. "It sucks to be you," said Tim.*

empire *n.* a type of government acceptable only when it is ancient or privately owned.

employee *n.* someone who understands that the boss wants suggestions to improve the company, not her personality.

encourage *v.* **1.** to egg someone on by not rejecting him. **2.** to support the career paths, personal decisions, and peculiar habits of loved ones.

enemy *n.* someone who once made you angry, and you never managed to tell them so.

engagement *n.* a good term to use if you're trying to break up with someone you're dating. *See REVERSE PSYCHOLOGY.*

engenderment *n.* the process of turning into a boy or a girl. Anyone confused should pick a gender and run with it.

enjoy *v.* to derive pleasure; to revel in an experience; to live in the moment.

enraged *adj.* beyond angry, due to frustration residue.

enterprise *n.* **1.** a business undertaking. **2.** the quality that makes one undertake an undertaking.

equivocate *v.* to waver between indecision and desire.

erogenous *adj.* a zone where men get lost because of their refusal to ask for directions.

erotic *adj.* sexual in a heightened, literary, or peculiar way. *In Bubbles's e-mail to Steve, she wrote that she found soft, unattached earlobes especially erotic.*

eroticize *v.* to translate into the language of love.

encourage *v.* the male equivalent of "nurture."

enemy *n.* person who wants something you have, or has something you want.

engagement *n.* a battle. *The engagement at Okinawa resulted in heavy losses.*

engenderment *n.* the process of becoming a man. You'll find out how well you're doing at your eulogy.

enjoy *v.* what the waiter who wants to show good intentions may invite you to do with your food.

enraged *adj.* pissed off, big-time. To enrage a man, insult his mother. Or blame him for not doing something he didn't know he was supposed to do. To really enrage him, do the blame thing, and <u>be</u> his mother.

enterprise *n.* the motivation to boldly go where no one has gone before, or at least not recently. Like Pluto, or Topeka.

equivocate *v.* having started strong and sounded resolute, to realize suddenly the implications of what you just said and start to cover it over as best you can without retracting it, exactly.

erogenous *adj.* a zone where women get lost because of their reluctance to give directions.

erotic *adj.* sexy. *For Steve, even the phrase "fleshy earlobes" was erotic.*

eroticize *v.* to find erotic properties in an object that seems to have none; the principal task of adolescence. Like when you hump a sofa.

eternity *n.* the amount of time spent waiting in line when you have to be somewhere else.

euphemism *n.* a gentle characterization, lately inclined toward political correctness. "Horizontally challenged" is a euphemism for "fat." Euphemisms usually do not fully express the situation at hand. "Thoughtless" is a euphemism; *see* EVIL.

everyone *n.* those people who are used as evidence for underwhelming arguments. *"But everyone's into nipple-piercing now."*

evil *adj.* thoughtless, absent, or aloof.

ex *n.* someone who is always spoken about in the past tense, even when still alive. *"You smoke? My 'ex' smoked."* — The "ex" has neither died nor given up smoking, he has simply ceased to exist on a certain abstract level.

exaggeration *n.* a pastime invented by early hunters in their description of the woolly mammoth that got away. Since then, men have exaggerated the size and scope of most everything around them, with few repercussions and a surprising amount of success. Women are less prone to exaggerate, since we are more adoring of the accurate transmission of lovable details.

exercise *n.* **1.** an activity intended to make you a few sizes smaller. **2.** any ritualized process without hope. *An exercise in futility.*

exhibitionist *n.* a person who feels that clothes get in the way of things. Easy to find on beaches, on the stages of certain theaters, and in health clubs. It's hard to say whether the workout craze created more exhibitionists or simply got them all together in the same place, but this way it's more convenient for everyone involved.

eternity *n.* the amount of time that goes by between one's first sexual encounter and one's second.

euphemism *n.* polite phrase, the sexual implications of which may be denied. *"Gosh, that's a nice dress, Susan,"* for example, or *"Camilla, I wish I were your tampon." —Prince Charles.*

everyone *n.* those people who are out having sex while you're home alone.

evil *adj.* women who cheat—unless they are cheating with you.

ex *n.* **1.** a woman you dumped, after you realized you didn't like her. **2.** a woman who dumped you, before you realized you didn't like her.

exaggeration *n.* act of overstating the truth, as when trying to convince a dating prospect or a game warden that an entity is twelve inches long.

exercise *n.* **1.** an activity intended to make you a few sizes bigger. **2.** an activity intended to help others feel a few sizes smaller.

exhibitionist *n.* someone who shows parts of him- or herself to people who don't want to see them. If people want to see them, the exhibitor is known as a "model."

exotic *adj.* describes a type of vacation.

expect *v.* to tell all your friends that something desirable will happen.

expectation *n.* how you imagine things will turn out, only to be disappointed later. *Jan had once had expectations that Lloyd would be a nurturing father because he was so good about watering the plants.*

expecting *adj.* pregnant. Applies only to women, despite men who try to get in on the fun by announcing, "We're expecting."

experience *n.* a supposed but ineffective source of knowledge. Immanuel Kant said you couldn't learn from experience, probably because he didn't have any himself. *(See VIRGIN.)* Lord Byron, who slept with anything that moved, said, "I learned everything from experience, that's why I know nothing." It's not impossible to learn from experience—it's just that repeating past mistakes is irresistible.

explore *v.* to probe about. Explorers used to kill natives and ravish their lands. Today it is fashionable to explore without exploiting. Women are good at post-colonial exploration, because we enjoy analyzing people and always try to put things back where we found them.

expose *v.* **1.** to reveal too much about someone else's duplicity, which can get you into trouble. **2.** to show too much flesh, which can also get you into trouble.

exotic *adj.* describes a type of dancer.

expect *v.* to believe that someone should know you well enough to do this one lousy thing without your having to say what it is.

expectation *n.* what people feel they get to have, without limit, as long as they tell you in advance. *"I have high expectations for you in this basketball game,"* Lloyd told his son, shortly after explaining what basketball was.

expecting *v.* pregnant. Not to be confused with expectorating.

experience *n.* whatever someone lives through.

explore *v.* a primal urge. A way to see and feel new things and people. A way to prepare against danger, to learn by risking. It is possible to explore emotions, but most men are not rewarded for that while young and never learn the skills.

expose *v.* to open one's financial dealings, or one's raincoat.

F

ON FISHING

Rooting for a nightcrawler amid mud, pulling it out for an appraisal, and impaling it on a barbed metal hook so that it is likely neither to die immediately nor to disintegrate during your cast—these activities have long kept fishing male.

The liberation of women, however, has led many to give fishing a try, whenever an unliberated man can be found to bait the hook. With the arrival of women, rules prohibiting conversation aboard boat or ashore—based on an untested hunch that such talk "scares the fish"—have been eased. It is now conceded that passing waterskiers pose more of a threat than words spoken above the surface.

And so men, who could once stare for silent hours at the place where their line met its watery reflection, feel a need to retreat still further. They can no longer count on fishing for a sedentary peace.

But an active peace remains, in the gurgling streams of the trout.

True, you can no longer sit still and pretend you are

F

fable *n.* a tale with a moral. The only ones you need to know are the ant and the grasshopper (keep a savings account), the tortoise and the hare (quietly persevere and you'll triumph over obnoxious people), and the fox and the grapes (dieting is good).

doing something. You also lose the need for worms. (When you used worms, you might not have caught a fish all day, but at least you knew you'd killed something.)

Trout fishing has other rewards. It enables the married or committed man to exercise his instincts, and stay in the hunt. All he has to do is change the object of his chase, from a woman to a fish.

He needs extra equipment—hip waders, a special pole, lures that are supposed to look like flies. A rumpled, vaguely dirty vest and a floppy hat earn extra credit.

Looking like this, he is ready to seduce a trout:

- He must "present" the lure gently, so as not to frighten. That means a practiced cast, and (always important) you can tell a novice from an expert by his cast.
- The smaller his hook, the more skill he needs to catch anything.
- The fight a fish puts up is a measure of its worth.
- A man's skill is measured by how many he can catch.
- What he catches, he generally doesn't keep. Commitment is not only unnecessary—it is discouraged, so other fishermen can share the delight. A trout-fishing bumper sticker reads, "Love 'em and Leave 'em."

Only the novice wants to keep what he catches.

F

fable *n.* a tale with a moral. The only ones you need to know are the ant and the grasshopper (work hard or you'll die), the tortoise and the hare (if you relax you'll lose everything), and the fox and the grapes (a woman who won't go out with you may still be sweet).

fabulous *adj.* full of élan. Can apply to personality, fashion choices, or moral behavior.

fact *n.* an indisputable opinion. Winter is longer than summer. People with hips should avoid shirtdresses. Jane Austen rules.

failure *n.* the inability to communicate.

faint *v.* to swoon; to collapse in a heap. Once a popular social tool for expressing outrage, surprise, or guilt, fainting has gone the way of the corset and is now reserved for the truly deoxygenated.

faith *n.* an irrational belief based on warm, loving feelings. *Steve, an incurable romantic, had faith that Melinda would look great in a shirtdress.*

fake *adj.* to simulate a better reality than the one you know. *Anne told Lloyd she had only faked three times with him.*

fall **1.** *n.* the rejuvenating autumn months, when one considers shopping for new wardrobe items, school courses, and romantic interests. **2.** *v.* to career into a void, such as a ravine, a mine shaft, or a state of ecstatic love. **3.** *n. The Fall:* when Adam and Eve were forced to leave Eden after straying from God's diet plans. Although it's known as the "Fall of Man," women are inevitably blamed for it. No one points out that God was encouraging the first eating disorder with His unrealistic attitude toward forbidden fruit and punishment.

false **1.** *adj.* untrue. *But Anne's statement was false.* **2.** *adj.* unreal. *But Jan's eyelashes were false.*

fabulous *adj.* super. A word that, if you say it, no matter how much it fits, makes you a little . . . suspect, if you know what I mean. (A gutsy move, in a homophobic world.)

fact *n.* an indisputable opinion. The Earth is round. Space is big. The best quarterback ever was Joe Montana.

failure *n.* the inability to perform.

faint *adj.* hard to discern. *He heard a faint cry for help, and, unsure of its meaning, he ignored it.*

faith *n.* a stubborn belief based on no facts whatsoever. *Melinda, a Miami native, had faith that Dan Marino was as good as Montana.*

fake *v.* a thing men do with love, so we won't have to do it with sex. *Lloyd told himself he had only faked three months with Anne.*

fall *v.* to sink or droop. *Steve, sitting attentively at the front of church, hoped his manhood would fall before he had to rise.*

false *adj.* **1.** misleading. As in a toupee or plastic fingernails. **2.** in football, an improper play, which is penalized: *false start.* **3.** in a relationship, an improper play, which may be penalized: *For Lloyd, being false to Anne felt true.*

family *n.* people who offer one love and opinions without provocation.

fancy *adj.* formal. It is always better to err on the side of fancy. Then those around you can feel underdressed and insecure, instead of the other way around.

fantasy *n.* a plausible dream scenario involving people you know. Distinguished from reality only in that it hasn't happened yet.

fart *v.* to express flatulence and alienate friends.

fashion *n.* a way of expressing oneself daily—or more frequently if one changes outfits often enough. *Fashion industry:* a business that dresses the insecure and anticipates the seasons. Other than corrupting the tradition of the Gregorian calendar and feeding the paranoias of the most impressionable anorexics, there is not much harm in it. *See* FAST.

fast *v.* to stop eating in order to accommodate a given religious holiday or fashion trend. Can lead to lightheadedness, low blood sugar, spiritual epiphany, or becoming a size four. Not recommended for anyone who is already a size four. *Feeling miserable, Jan glanced in the mirror and decided to fast.*

fat *adj.* anything that seems remotely bulging or round, even if only for a moment.

fate *n.* a force greater than oneself or other people; the reason that true love triumphs in a harsh world; an excellent guilty party to blame when love doesn't triumph.

father *n.* someone who hates your boyfriends even more than you do.

fault *n.* a personal flaw, best unmentioned until you're having an argument, when faults can be listed as helpful examples.

family *n.* group that keeps a man going to work, so he can pay them enough to leave him in peace.

fancy *adj.* containing "ruffles," "frills," and other nonsense.

fantasy *n.* as many wet, willing, beautiful strangers as you want, without a chance of guilt, pregnancy, or other disease.

fart *v.* to burp, from the other end.

fashion *v.* to make, as a cabinet.

fast *adj.* **1.** rapid. **2.** used to describe a woman who knows how to have a good time.

fat *adj.* **1.** a type of cell that stores excess energy. **2.** a person of size.

fate *n.* supernatural force that ensured you'd meet your wife, and your mistress.

father *n.* a man whose complete approval no son has ever won. This is good training for meeting the rest of the world.

fault *n.* **1.** a crack in the earth's crust where two continental plates rub against each other, causing quakes. **2.** cracks in your character, which rub against the nerves of your partner, also causing quakes.

faux pas *n.* literally "the wrong step." Any movement or word that confirms everyone's underlying suspicion that you are, at bottom, a nitwit.

fawn *v. to fawn upon:* to become sycophantic around; to buy gifts for; to have an infinite amount of patience with, until your attentions are returned.

fear *n.* the feeling that at any moment a lunatic will throw you on the sidewalk.

feature 1. *n.* a given physical attribute. 2. *v.* to display prominently. 3. *n.* a full-length film. *The actor's best features were featured in his last feature.*

feed *v.* 1. to nourish, unintentionally. *Lloyd had no idea how his comments would feed Anne's insecurities.* 2. to nourish, intentionally. *Anne sensed when Lloyd started feeding her the tortellini out of his palm that he still wanted her, and forgot about all those insecurities.*

feelings *n. pl.* the thoughts of the heart.

feminist *n.* anyone who knows that *Pretty Woman* was a movie that glamorized prostitution—and that Julia Roberts used a body double.

femme fatale *n.* a woman whose attractiveness is so devastating, it may cause death. These women do not come with Surgeon General's warnings attached; you just have to know.

fetish *n.* an obsession with a physical theme. Some etymologists believe that "fetish" and "feet" have the same root, which would explain why most men think of feet and most women think of shoes when the topic arises in polite conversation.

faux pas *n.* a social error. For example, to loudly pass gas in front of certain women. It's hard to make a faux pas in front of other men, although "Hey, Frank, your wife's got a great rack" comes close.

fawn 1. *n.* a young deer. **2.** *v.* the reaction of young women to young deer.

fear *n.* the feeling that at any moment someone will call you a sissy.

feature *n.* a part of someone or something, as in a stereo component, or a leg.

feed *v.* to gratify. *If this meal went on much longer, Lloyd would have to go out to the street and feed the meter.*

feelings *n. pl.* the disruptor beams of the brain.

feminist *n.* one who supports a woman's right to male privileges (volunteering for the military) without male responsibilities (getting drafted).

femme fatale *n.* a total babe for whom you wouldn't mind dying, even if she's the one who pulls the trigger.

fetish *n.* a perverse attraction, i.e., an attraction to anything other than the following: breasts, shoulders, legs, lips, eyes, noses, cheeks, genitals, arms, buttocks, navels, backs, hands, sports cars, leather, cold cash, fresh linen, or foreign accents.

fiancé(e) *n.* a word that indicates the poverty of the English language. In order to say you are a person planning to get married, you have to say it in French.

fiasco *n.* **1.** a disaster. **2.** a wine bottle with a basketlike covering. **3.** a disaster involving drinking out of too many wine bottles with basketlike coverings.

fierce *adj.* having sharp teeth or strong words.

finally *adv.* what you say to a man when he comes to his senses.

firm *adj.* a word that should describe as many parts of one's body as possible for as many years as possible.

firm up *v.* to confirm the existence of, as in a crucial appointment or a favorite body part.

first base *n.* **1.** a stolen kiss. **2.** an end in itself.

first date 1. *n.* a preliminary encounter. **2.** *adj.* any choice preceding said encounter that is calculated to make a great first impression: *a first-date smile.*

first mate *n.* **1.** a sailor who doesn't run the ship but could if the need arose. Like Gilligan. **2.** an initial reproductive partner.

first move, the *n.* a historically nerve-wracking proposition, turned by recent havoc and legislation into a total nightmare. Now he has to ask you, you have to verbalize your lust for him, and he needs a permission slip signed by your doctor and co-op board. If overwhelmed by the bureaucracy of foreplay, make this yourself.

fishing *n.* a sport men love because they can get dinner and torture worms at the same time.

fiancé *n.* one who lacks the loneliness of the bachelor and the financial obligation of the husband.

fiasco *n.* an utter disaster—as in a condom breaking or the Knicks losing in the last minute of play.

fierce *adj.* at least as strong as you are, and angrier.

finally *adv.* what you should never say to a woman who has just agreed to go to bed with you.

firm *n.* a parasitical organism of law or business, which maintains itself by calling its new hosts "partners" and making their fate inseparable from its own.

firm up *v.* to add cement.

first base *n.* **1.** the one even Rickey Henderson couldn't steal. **2.** a means to an end.

first date *n.* your audition—a time of unmatched suspense which may change your life and your bank account.

first mate *n.* **1.** the captain's pinch hitter. Like Spock. **2.** an initial wife.

first move, the *n.* a full-on kiss, with tongue. Still the man's obligation, if he wants what may come next. The woman who thinks she made the first move often means she made it OBVIOUS that he should kiss her.

fishing *v.* what men do silently, for cold, aquatic creatures. What women do loudly, for warm, fuzzy compliments. The quiet activity requires a license.

fix up *v.* to realize that two people you know belong together before they realize it.

fixate *v.* to obsess about; to be unable to remove one's eyes from. *When Melinda met Steve, she couldn't help fixating on his tie right away: the pattern was so distracting and it clashed with his shirt.*

flaky *adj.* impossibly vague. As women have achieved greater responsibility in traditional society, men, exhausted from dominating for centuries, have grown more flaky. Fortunately for them, men who are flaky are often referred to instead as "theoretically gifted."

flare *v.* **1.** to enlarge around the edges, as certain skirts and nostrils do when provoked. **2.** *to flare up:* to explode and yell mean things. *Melinda hoped Steve wouldn't flare up when she told him the truth.*

flat tire *n.* the one thing men are good at changing.

flexible *adj.* **1.** thrilled at the idea of changing course to accommodate others. **2.** skilled at doing splits.

flimsy *adj.* easily proven wrong. *Lloyd gave Jan a flimsy excuse about where he had been.*

fling *n.* any sexual relationship lasting less than a week.

fix up *v.* to repair, as a TV antenna.

fixate *v.* to obsess on an object. Men on sex, women on . . . whatever. *Steve fixated on the fact that Melinda kept looking at his chest. Was this a sign?*

flaky *adj.* describes someone who can't say "no," or even "yes." Hence, an exciting date, but a tiresome girlfriend.

flare *n.* what you ignite when your car breaks down.

flat tire *n.* **1.** deflated rubber tube that someone, usually a man, must fix. **2.** a discombobulation produced by stepping on the back of someone's shoe, so his foot pops out and crushes the back of the shoe on the next step. Fun at slow parties.

flexible *adj.* what a woman asks you to be when you've been foolish enough to tell her you don't want to do what she wants you to want to do. *"Can't you be more flexible?" Jan asked Lloyd when he declined her subtle invitation to the museum. Lloyd decided no, he couldn't be.*

flimsy *adj.* easily pushed aside. *Lloyd had been buying some flimsy lingerie for Anne.*

fling *v.* to throw, as a Frisbee.

flip *v.* to flip—to freak out, to crumble under duress, to lose it. *Jan flipped when she heard Lloyd's excuse.* **2.** to turn over, as in cooking. *Jan flipped the pancakes expertly when she heard Lloyd's excuse, so expertly that he did not notice she had flipped.* **3.** to toss to the side, as in hair. *Jan was sure that Lloyd's mistress was the redhead she saw at his office party, the type who in grade school would have sat with those girls who flipped their hair in sync during assembly.* **4.** *adj.* dry, sardonic, nonchalant. *Jan tried to think of something flip to say, but nothing came to mind.*

flirtation *n.* the process of expressing one's attraction to people by getting them more interested in you than you are in them.

floozy *n.* what a bimbo turns into at night.

food *n.* a source of obsession; a source of comfort; a source of calories.

force 1. *n.* gravitational pull or intellectual strength. **2.** *v. to force an issue*: to cause a decision to be made by glaring at someone.

forget *v.* to experience memory lapse. Like denial, only more efficient.

forgive *v.* to let bygones be bygones. Saints are good at this.

formal *adj.* **1.** clothing that can make anyone seem good-looking. **2.** the repression of emotions, as in Emily Dickinson's observation: *"After great pain, a formal feeling comes."*

forward *adj.* **1.** uninhibited, bold, or intoxicated. **2.** in a forward-moving direction. *The women's movement crept forward slowly.*

frank *adj.* what people ask you for permission to be before they insult you.

flip *v.* to display, as a finger. *Lloyd had an unaccountable impulse to flip Jan the bird.*

flirtation *n.* a platonic affair. Occasionally followed by the Aristotelian kind.

floozy *n.* a woman who enjoys sex enough to have it for free.

food *n.* **1.** source of sustenance. **2.** source of pleasure. **3.** source of energy, enabling you to work long enough to afford more sustenance.

force 1. *n.* physical power. **2.** *v.* *to force an issue*: to cause a decision to be made by showing a weapon.

forget *v.* what people really want you to do when they ask you to forgive.

forgive *v.* to make your anger less obvious.

formal *n.* a dance or dinner where the men try to look the same and the women try not to.

forward *adj.* where you should always say your relationship is heading.

frank *n.* a hot dog.

free *adj.* able to say or do whatever one wants.

freedom *n.* the knowledge that one can choose to do what one pleases in a variety of arenas. Has nothing to do with trekking around or even leaving the house. May involve decorating the house.

friend *n.* a person who consoles you or shares your joy; who accompanies you on fruitless missions; who borrows things but returns them promptly.

friendly *adj.* effusive, communicative, open. Anyone who mistakes friendly for flirty should get a life. *See* FRIEND.

fruity *adj.* **1.** sugary; having an artificial flavor or a sweet fragrance. **2.** eccentric.

frumpy *adj.* when your clothes are twenty years older than you are.

frustration *n.* the discovery that not everyone shares your world view.

fun *n.* joy or amusement, no matter how perverse. *Phoebe always introduced her ex-husbands to each other at parties, because she thought it would be fun.*

funny *adj.* **1.** entertaining. *"That's not funny."* **2.** strange. *After Steve told Melinda the joke he thought was funny, she had a funny look on her face.*

future *n.* **1.** a time in one's career that fascinates men, who want to know where one plans to be then instead of where one is now. **2.** a time in all relationships when problems suddenly vanish. **3.** a time in that special relationship to think about on the first date and start planning by the third.

free *adj.* able to see or do whomever one wants.

freedom *n.* the illusion that your behavior is not constrained by society. Fostered by alcohol.

friend *n.* a person to whom you try not to complain—but when you do, he knows just what you mean.

friendly *adj.* warm and open. Not the masculine ideal. A man who is "friendly" is trying to prove that he's different from other men. Don't believe him.

fruity *adj.* probably gay.

frumpy *adj.* fat, old, dowdy, or otherwise unappealing.

frustration *n.* the experience of not having gotten what you wanted.

fun *n.* a source of endorphins. *Describing her bedroom habits to Phoebe's current husband was the ex-husbands' idea of fun.*

funny *adj.* **1.** causing laughter, because entertaining. *"Yes, it is, it's totally funny."* **2.** causing laughter, because embarrassing. *Steve laughed, explaining how funny he found it that he had tried that joke on three women, none of whom laughed, while men seemed to find it hilarious. Melinda's funny look remained.*

future *n.* **1.** the time by which you will be closer to death, if not already there. **2.** a time that has by definition not arrived. And I won't know how I'll feel then about this relationship until it *does* arrive. So there.

G

games *n. pl.* things people play until one person gets bored and lets the other one win.

garters *n. pl.* lacy, itchy hosiery attachments that ought to be worn sparingly, and only in situations where one feels guaranteed that one will be disrobing shortly. *After her marriage fell apart, Jan started wearing garters in order to feel attractive, ate lots of fried food, and developed a sudden crush on her co-worker Boris.*

gay *adj.* attracted to members of the same sex. May confuse members of the opposite sex. *When Boris told Jan he was gay, she decided not to ask him out after all.*

gaze *n.* a meaningful look. There is the two-way gaze, better known as "eyelock," and there is the one-way gaze—really a failed two-way gaze in which the gazee is unimpressed. Still, as Mae West noted, "It is better to be looked over than overlooked."

gender-neutral *adj.* the biggest faux pas of the equal rights movement, when having a boy or girl became replaced by the chic practice of having an "it." While the studies are amusing to read about, it is not suggested that one try it on one's own children.

genderalization *n.* a generalization about gender. Becoming more and more popular, as people discover they are true.

gentle *adj.* wonderfully tender and sweet. *Boris gave Tim a gentle caress by the watercooler, and Jan understood there was no hope.*

G

games *n. pl.* things people play to find out who is best.

garters *n. pl.* little-used nowadays. But it's worth renting *Bull Durham* to learn how to undo them, just in case.

gay *adj.* **1.** attracted to members of the same sex. This attraction often worries non-gay members of that sex, who think gays must all be attracted to them. They flatter themselves. **2.** *archaic.* carefree.

gaze *n.* a steady look gay men, when looking at another man, often hold longer than straight men—thus, a means of recognition. Straight men tend to look at other men for shorter periods, which makes the other men easier to kill. (Which is why generals don't want gaze in the military.)

gender-neutral *adj.* any barbershop that calls itself a "salon," where the barber calls himself a "stylist" and offers "body waves."

genderalization *n.* an assessment based on the theory that genitals mean everything.

gentle *adj.* good for a man to be, in bed. But bad for him to appear, out of bed, unless he also has money or just wants to be friends.

gentleman *n*. an old-fashioned man, who opens doors for women because he respects them and also to get a better view of them from behind.

get *v*. **1.** to purchase, on a whim. **2.** to understand, on a deep level.

glove *n*. a prop; in Victorian times, you could drop one on the floor to see who liked you enough to pick it up. Contemporary women do not drop gloves. We drop hints.

God *n*. is supposed to be constantly present, all-forgiving, understanding, the source of life—and <u>male</u>. All of these things would be much easier to believe if he were female, or at least an androgynous cloud-animal of some kind.

goddess *n*. **1.** a female deity, overflowing with fruit and benevolence. **2.** a woman so desired and worshiped that she can have any man she wants— though that man will probably be afraid to talk to her.

good *adj*. **1.** angelic. *Jan was raised to be a good girl.* **2.** enjoyable. *Nonetheless, Jan enjoyed a good lay.* **3.** promising. *Jan thought the weather forecast looked good; it would rain on the day of her annulment.*

goofball *n*. a nutty individual who has managed to become a part of your life. (This is probably your own fault.)

gossip *n*. a way of discussing the nature of life and being, in the guise of discussing other people's lives.

graceful *adj*. delicate and sweeping, without stumbling, falling, or taking up too much room.

grandfather *n*. a man who is supposed to dispense wisdom but is just as likely to dispense junk food.

gentleman *n*. **1.** a man who opens a door for a woman. **2.** a man who does not open a door for a woman.

get *v*. to obtain, as in to grab.

glove *n*. object worn around the hand as protection, making it easier to catch a baseball, swing a golf club, or commit murder.

God *n*. The Big Guy, the Head Honcho, Numero Uno. Figure out what He doesn't want you to do, and then don't do it. (If He's a She, you're in more trouble than you thought.)

goddess *n*. **1.** Cindy Crawford. **2.** Claudia Schiffer.

good *adj*. acceptable. *The Red Sox beat the Yankees by a good margin.*

goofball *n*. an entertaining nonconformist who seems harmless. *"Todd, you're, like, a total goofball."*

gossip *v*. a way of comparing your life to that of someone who is not there, and deciding yours is better.

graceful *adj*. thin.

grandfather *n*. an alternate role model, in case you don't want to be *exactly* like your dad.

grandmother *n.* someone you turn into while you'r too busy focusing on not turning into your mother.

grate *v.* to shred by friction. *Anne, hoping to get Lloyd grate the cheese, told him how good Paul had been grating cheese.*

greedy *adj.* desiring attention.

grind *v.* to sharpen vigorously to make yourself feel bette

groom 1. *n.* The great-looking guy on top of the wee ding cake. **2.** *v.* to make oneself better-looking in ca one ever needs to stand on top of a wedding cake.

grope *v.* to search for the right word or idea.

grounded *adj.* in touch with reality, as are women those who tell the boss how a project really is goin; Men prefer saying how the project *could* be going— they are driven by a need to float beyond earth things that they consider annoying. Women, consid ered floatier, are actually far more grounded.

guess *v.* to suddenly realize how much you know.

guest *n.* someone who shows up when invited an brings a gift nice enough to be useful but not so ela orate that a thank-you note becomes necessary.

guilt *n.* a feeling that one has done something wron; even if one hasn't done it.

guilty *n.* awash with mental self-flagellation. *Feeling te ribly guilty, Melinda told Steve the truth: that she w actually Bubbles, too.*

grandmother *n.* a wonderful woman, who supports your explorations while worrying that the next Great Depression will swamp you.

grate *v.* to shred by friction. *Anne's talk of former lovers had begun to grate on Lloyd's nerves.*

greedy *adj.* desiring more than someone else thinks you need.

grind *v.* to undulate in a sexual manner: *"She said, 'How'd you like to waste some time?'/And I could not resist, when I saw little Nikki grind."*—The Artist Then Known As Prince.

groom **1.** *n.* a man who cares for several horses, or one woman. **2.** *v.* to pick bugs out of an animal's fur.

grope *v.* to fumble around for an object indifferent to your search.

grounded *adj.* a word of shifting significance. When a ball is intentionally grounded in football, a penalty ensues. Theories and neurotics, on the other hand, *should* be grounded, while a teenager would just as soon not be. Finally, it's good for a high-voltage wire to be grounded, except when it's grounded through you.

guess *n.* to subtly conceal how little you know.

guest *n.* a much easier role than "host"—you don't have to clean anything but your clothes, you don't have to keep the conversation flowing, and you can leave.

guilt *n.* a feeling that one has done something wrong, even if one wasn't caught.

guilty *adj.* deserving of actual flagellation.

gullible *adj*. highly impressionable; a state nourished b[...]
love.

gurgle *n*. a pathetic glugging noise made by inarticula[...]
individuals. Only acceptable in babies, whose spit bu[...]
bles can sound so lilting that one is tempted to go o[...]
maternity leave just to listen to them for a time.

guru *n*. a spiritual leader. Once restricted to religio[...]
gurus now dominate nutrition, weight-lifting, and int[...]
rior design.

gush *v*. to go on and on about wonderful, cute things[...]

gut *n*. in its singular form, means the seat of intuition. *S[...]*
could feel in her gut that it wasn't going to work out. [...]
its plural form, the gut doubles as the location [...]
courage. *But she didn't know if she was going to ha[...]*
the guts to say so.

guy *n*. a term once reserved for a friendly compete[...]
man, until women realized they had no equivalent an[...]
took the plural form for themselves. So it is now lik[...]
ly for a woman to say to a group of her girlfriends [...]
have to tell you guys something" if she's being seriou[...]
If she's being sarcastic, she'll still say, "I have to te[...]
you girls something." That's just how it is.

gynecocracy *n*. Government by women, which woul[...]
be incredibly efficient. As Margaret Thatcher noted, "[...]
politics, if you want something said, ask a man. If yo[...]
want something done, ask a woman."

gullible *adj.* prone to trust. *Melinda looked suitably guilty, but Steve still felt gullible; he wondered if her name was really Melinda.*

gurgle *n.* sound made by persons so angry they're choking on their own bile, so sick they're choking on their own blood, or so young they're having trouble with saliva.

guru *n.* someone who knows what God wants you to give your guru.

gush *v.* something you want an oil well to start doing, and a crying woman to stop doing.

gut *n.* in its singular form, a paunch. *She had quite a gut.* In its plural form, reservoirs of courage. *But he didn't have the guts to point that out.*

guy *n.* a man without pretensions. Warning: when someone says *"Hey, I'm just an ordinary guy,"* run.

gynecocracy *n.* government run by doctors who specialize in "women's issues."

H

History of The Male and Female Languages

Like Hungarian and Finnish, French and Portuguese, Sanskrit and Latin, the Male and Female languages have common roots. In fact they started out as one language thousands of years ago. But early on, Eve and Adam stopped being able to agree on names for anything, and the two languages have been going in separate directions.

H

habituation *n.* the state of having grown accustomed to a situation until it begins to molder. Not good for romance, because romance doesn't molder very well.

had *v.* manipulated. *Melinda hoped Steve wouldn't feel had.*

hair *n.* the physical feature that sets the tone for the day.

hairline *n.* the one body part women worry about less than men.

hairstyle *n.* a situation to change constantly if you're a public figure who wants people to think well of you or a private one who feels restless. When you're at peace with yourself, any hairstyle will do.

ever since. Adam liked words to be as long as possible; Eve enjoyed abbreviations. Eve strung together longer sentences, while Adam glared at her to get to the point.

Both languages began as a way of expressing eternal truths. Then they ran into a few obstacles, like Adam, Eve, hormones, oppression by the fashion industry, and theoretical thinking. The revelation of modernism was that one truth lay in art. The revelation of postmodernism was that several truths lay in politics. The revelation of this book is that there is one great truth, but girls and boys have different words for it. Which leaves us both wondering what that truth may be.

—JLB

H

habituation *n*. the state of having grown so accustomed to a stimulus ("Lloyd, can you PLEASE take out the garbage?") that it no longer evokes anxiety (or action).

had *v*. to have experienced sexual intercourse with. *Steve knew he'd feel fine, once he'd had Melinda.*

hair *n*. what you want on your chest, as a teenager. As an adult, you want it back on your head.

hairline *n*. like love, a thing you take for granted until it recedes.

hairstyle *n*. what hairdressers and women call a haircut.

half *n*. One of two equal parts of a whole. *Other half:* significant other. This term comes from Plato's theory that men and women were originally one creature who split in two, and are now condemned to spend our lives looking for the person who used to be attached to us. A flawed theory. (Plato clearly didn't date much, because then he would have known you have to be complete by yourself first before you can bear to meet anyone else.)

hand *n*. willingness to become someone's spouse. *He asked for her hand.* (Gender-specific. Although women do propose to men, we never ask for their "hand." Perhaps because it's less likely to be manicured.)

handholding *n*. an indication of mutual regard and trust; a bonding experience.

handsome *adj*. describes a man who's fun to look at but not fun to date.

hapless *adj*. impossible to offend. Hapless people do not understand signals that they should leave you alone, like not returning their calls or walking backward when you run into them.

happened *v*. a soothing, karmic explanation for anything. *I don't know, it just happened.*

happiness *n*. the attainment of bliss.

happy *adj*. **1.** anxiety-free, successful, and desired. **2.** capable of giving and receiving love.

hate *n*. what love turns into when it sours. Sort of like mayonnaise turning into green mold, but more alarming. Try to clean out the fridge first.

have *v*. to possess, for the rest of time. *Melinda had to have Steve.*

half *n.* **1.** fifty percent. **2.** *Better half:* How a man refers to his wife, relieved that she has taken on the dirty work of being kind and considerate. This frees him to follow his instincts.

hand *n.* a tool for getting what you want, until you find a spouse.

handholding *n.* helping someone who isn't doing his job.

handsome *adj.* appealing to women. Those whose faces are not handsome may feel impelled to earn a handsome salary.

hapless *adj.* lacking hap. ("Hap" is Spanish for "clue.")

happened *v.* a shoddy way to avoid responsibility. *"What do you mean, 'It just happened'?"*

happiness *n.* the absence of misery.

happy *adj.* **1.** inebriated. **2.** (*more advanced*) capable of receiving and withholding love.

hate *n.* what you feel toward people when they think they're better than you are—and you agree.

have *v.* to possess, for the rest of the afternoon. *If Melinda was also Bubbles, Steve just had to have them. Uh, her.*

headache *n.* sinus pain caused by stress, flu, or too much TV. Relieved by aspirin or love letters.

health *n.* **1.** physical vigor and soundness, caused by buying exercise tapes, eating cantaloupe, and drinking diet soda. **2.** mental soundness: a sudden feeling of calm that involves dessert.

heart *n.* an organ crucial to love-making and decision-making.

heartbreak *n.* a state that occurs when someone has stomped all over your emotions and left them in a crumpled little pile. At least it means you have a functioning heart, which not everyone does. *See* HEARTLESS.

heartless *adj.* unfeeling, remorseless, cruel. Heartless behavior is usually in the eye of the beholder. *When Lloyd accused Anne of being heartless, she said no, she was just busy.*

heartthrob *n.* a man who prefers a mirror to a conversation.

heels *n. pl.* shoe adjuncts that strengthen your calf muscles, make you taller, incite passion, and ultimately destroy your ligaments and your ability to wear sneakers.

heliolatry *n.* sun worship. Practiced by ancient Egyptians and recent Californians. As in all religions, there is a trade-off. But instead of giving up fun now to get to paradise later, you get the paradise first and wrinkles and melanoma afterward.

hell *n.* supposedly a place of fires and damnation, but actually an emotional experience. Any location can become a personal hell. Milton said, *"The mind is its own place, and in itself, can make a heaven of hell, a hell of heaven."* Milton knew what he was talking about.

headache *n.* any obstacle to happiness.

health *n.* the absence of disease. May include a sense of well-being, if you're not part of Western culture.

heart *n.* the part of your body that pumps the blood and quits when it gets clogged.

heartbreak *n.* a state that occurs when the person by whom you set your inner clock breaks away and you can't remember how, or why, to reset it.

heartless *adj.* what a woman proves herself to be when she doesn't give you what you want. The prettier she is, the more likely you are to notice this quality.

heartthrob *n.* a male celebrity women find attractive.

heels *n. pl.* **1.** an aphrodisiac right up there with the low-cut blouse and the miniskirt. **2.** what women used to call the men who responded to such signals by salivating.

heliolatry *n.* the worship of blondes.

hell *n.* **1.** a loneliness too profound to discuss, for fear of showing weakness or a lack of independence. **2.** the state of having a penis and no place to put it.

hero *n.* an ideal specimen of manhood, as exemplified by the feats of the heroic age in the fifth century BC. They just don't make 'em like they used to.

heroine *n.* a woman whose sacrifice of everything is actually noted.

herstory *n.* a hip, quasi-feminist way to say "history." A term considered by some to have a male bias, since it contains the word "his"; but in actuality, "history" derives from the French word for "story"—*"histoire"*—while "herstory" sounds suspiciously like "her store." If you want to be sexually correct, there are better words to choose from.

hexaemeron *n.* the six days of creation. God was so efficient in that brief time that many others have since been inspired to leave huge amounts of work till the last minute.

high **1.** *n.* a peak that balances a low. **2.** *adj.* on drugs or inexplicably happy without them.

hint *n.* a wonderfully understated suggestion. Understanding hints, no matter how delicate, is a sign of pure intelligence.

hip **1.** *adj.* trendy; cool; whatever the latest thing is. **2.** *n.* an emblem of womanhood, fertility, and understanding how to use a belt.

his *adj.* **1.** anything belonging to him, or anything he thinks belongs to him. **2.** in case of divorce, anything that's left when the proceedings are over.

history *n.* the story of the past, which may be either instructive or embarrassing, and tends to weigh a lot. George Eliot wrote, *"The happiest women, like the happiest nations, have no history."*

hobby *n.* a favorite sideline. *Impotent men were Phoebe's hobby.*

hero *n*. a prominent figure, with access to babes galore.

heroine *n*. a woman who is admired by women.

herstory *n*. a word invented to remind us that Ancient Rome was co-ed.

hexaemeron *n*. proof that even God takes Sundays off to watch football.

high 1. *n*. a peak that leads to a low. **2.** *adj*. manic.

hint *n*. a form of communication that allows the recipient to guess what is wanted. To hint is a sign of weakness. A general does not give his colonel a hint.

hip *n*. Something cool to hold on to, or to watch as it walks away.

his *adj*. anything belonging to another man, until it becomes "yours."

history *n*. the record of traceable public occurrences, and theories of their influence. Henry Ford said, *"History is bunk."* But Henry Ford is now history. By his own admission, then Henry Ford is bunk.

hobby *n*. an activity that gives meaning to free time. *Lloyd admitted to himself that his favorite hobby was adultery.*

hold *v.* to grasp, tightly, as if you never want to let go
2. *n.* *on hold:* a state of limbo. **3.** *to put on hold:* a tech
nique used by indecisive shoppers. *Phoebe couldn*
decide whether the skirt was too short to wear in fron
of her psychoanalysis patients, so she asked the sales
man to put it on hold.

homosexual *n.* a man who loves men but completely
understands women, probably because he knows wha
it's like to love men.

honesty *n.* not the best policy. If you want to get you
lover out of the house, give him wedding ultimatums
If you want him to commit, tell him you're feeling
pangs of lust for your friend Hal. Hal does not have to
be a real person.

hope *n.* **1.** what keeps us going when we would other
wise flounder. **2.** what keeps us in denial when we
would otherwise mature.

horripilation *n.* goosebumps. *Suzanne sometimes won*
dered if horripilation was the same as love, and how ol
she would have to be before she found out.

hot *adj.* **1.** extremely warm. **2.** unremittingly attractive
Both kinds can lead to unpleasant amounts of sweating

househusband *n.* a man who cooks, cleans, sews, and
takes care of the kids while his spouse pursues he
wordly ambitions. Does not have to wear an apron, bu
usually does so in the movies.

housewife *n.* an unsalaried, overworked professiona
who manages a household and any mental stability i
may contain. Does the same chores as a househus
band, but receives less applause and congratulation.

hold 1. *n. on hold:* on the phone, a state in which you may put someone with whom you don't really want to talk. **2.** *v.* in person, what you do to someone with whom you don't only want to talk.

homosexual *n.* a woman who loves women and understands men all too well.

honesty *n.* not the best policy. If you tell a woman too soon of your fantasies about her, she'll never act them out. And if you tell her of your fantasies about others?—anyway, just don't.

hope *n.* the remainder, when you subtract reality from a person's opinions. Woody Allen said, *"Marriage is the death of hope";* all that's left is reality.

horripilation *n.* goosebumps, brought on in a woman by gentle caresses, and by jumping out from behind a wall and shouting, "Boo!" *Tony wondered if horripilation meant a woman loved him—and decided it probably did.*

hot *adj.* the type of woman who won't talk to you. If you test this out, and she continues not to talk, you get to call her "cold."

househusband *n.* a good deal. You stay home, eat, shop, and play with the kids. She deals with angry bosses, customers, and underlings, and pronounces herself "fulfilled." Try not to laugh; you'll blow everything.

housewife *n.* a female househusband.

housework *n.* unpaid domestic servitude. Depending on the woman, these chores can either be complete drudgery or a soothing process. You can tell by looking at her house which one it is. In any case, whether the place sparkles or whether she is doing the bare minimum to keep from starving, housework means chores involving lots of male objects (dusters, brooms, plungers) but few actual men.

hug *n.* an act boys can't tolerate, but men learn to master

human *adj.* the world's worst excuse. Don't say "I'm only human" unless you want your mate to leave you for an android. Humanity is just not an unusual enough character trait to make for a decent explanation.

humble *adj.* aware that boasting is distasteful.

hungry *adj.* empty—when food or tears seem the only options.

hunk *n.* in the early 1800s, this term referred to a fat or large person. Then some oversized men got together to rewrite a few dictionaries, and voilà—now it means a handsome man with a well-developed body.

hunting *v.* looking in a predatory way for items such as lost earrings or the right word. Hunting for men is no advisable because one only finds them when one is least expecting it. Not even Diana, goddess of the hunt, hunted for men. She turned them into animals first.

husband *n.* there are two sorts of husbands: someone who marries you and forsakes all others, or someone who marries someone else and forsakes you. Try to pay more attention to the former.

housework *n.* the labor of cleaning and maintaining a domicile. What professional men are now told they should equally share, while continuing to pay most of the mortgage.

hug *v.* to become snug, as in a car hugging a curb.

human *adj.* having the same desires as a chimpanzee, but a greater capacity for denial.

humble *adj.* aware that one has nothing to boast about.

hungry *adj.* ambitious—a state often brought on by an empty stomach.

hunk *n.* a thick wad, as of cheese or bread.

hunting *v.* **1.** the practice of stalking an animal—with respect for its natural grace and ability, and with a weapon created to destroy ability and shatter grace. **2.** an unfortunate metaphor for courtship.

husband *n.* There are two kinds of husbands: the kind of man who struggles to bankroll a wife and children, and the kind who does not. The first kind is now seen as "primitive."

hypocrite *n.* **1.** a man who tells a woman that work takes priority over everything, unless it's her work. **2.** one who tells you not to be self-conscious, but criticizes you constantly. **3.** one who doesn't pay attention to you but gets in a fistfight with anyone who does.

hysterical *adj.* crazed. Ever since the Greeks identified hysteria with the female sex organ, things have gone downhill. The Victorians thought removing the uterus would calm a nervous woman—hence the blood-chilling term "hysterectomy"—proving they were even dumber than the Greeks. They didn't notice that men have fits of hysteria, too, simply known by other names. Like "temper." Or "war."

hypocrite *n.* a woman who eats natural foods and wears unnatural hair spray.

hysterical *adj.* describes a woman who won't listen to your reason.

I

ignore *v.* to deprive someone of all love and attention, in hopes that he will go away. A technique that often backfires, as people inevitably become more amorous when ignored.

illicit sex *n.* sex so fun that it is illegal. Not to be confused with implicit sex.

illusionment *n.* the refusal to be disillusioned.

image *n.* an illustrated idea. *Melinda always had an image of how an assistant professor should look, which led her to buy the black antique lace-up boots.* Also: a reputation to keep polished. *Melinda hoped that the fact she was dating a student wouldn't hurt her image in the political science department or her chances for tenure.*

imagine *v.* to make yourself believe you are happier than you really are.

immutable *adj.* rigid; refusing to improve.

implicit sex *n.* when you're not doing it but you might as well be. Includes slam-dancing, dirty talk, and the Lambada.

important *adj.* brimming with significance, possibility, or hope.

impotent *adj.* literally: powerless. Figuratively: powerless to have sex. Also: literally powerless to have sex. It is important to have sympathy for the powerless. Otherwise they'll only get more powerless, not to mention resentful.

I

ignore *v.* to exercise one's right to refuse interaction.

illicit sex *n.* sex you could get shot for having, by either a father or a husband. If that's the price, make sure it's <u>good</u>.

illusionment *n.* the use of drugs.

image *n.* what you have to live up to, once you project it. Unemployment can interfere. Kurt Vonnegut said *"You are who you pretend to be,"* but to this should be added, *"until you get caught being someone else,"* as Jimmy Swaggart could attest.

imagine *v.* to make yourself believe you're bedding more women than you actually are.

immutable *adj.* rigid; refusing to relax.

implicit sex *n.* similar to real sex in the way that reserving an airplane ticket is similar to actually sitting on the damn plane.

important *adj.* relating to a promotion, or a championship game.

impotent *adj.* describes a state that the Pope and his priesthood may pray for, but all other men pray against.

impress *v.* to put one's most attractive qualities on bold display.

impulse *adj.* describes something that one needs to own or eat the moment one sees it.

incoherent *adj.* too upset to explain why you're upset.

incompatible *adj.* having a worldview so different that it is unnerving.

incompetent *adj.* inept or hopeless at a given discipline. *Jan hoped to have Lloyd declared mentally incompetent at their divorce proceedings.*

indecent *adj.* wearing too few clothes.

independence *n.* freedom from self-appointed advisers.

indirect *adj.* delightfully roundabout.

indulge *v.* to agree to an outlandish activity for the sake of love.

inevitable *adj.* unstoppable, like beachfront erosion, journalistic errata, and love for those who cannot return it.

inexpressible *adj.* when an experience or emotion is so sublime that it cannot be conveyed in words. But the truth is, most things are articulable, and few of them sublime.

infantilize *v.* to treat a loved one like an infant.

infatuation *n.* a spurt of insanity that makes you think a total stranger has qualities that he doesn't actually have.

impress *v.* to provoke admiration. A man may try to compensate for a lack of beauty with money or boasts. Without them he feels naked, and the object of his desire stays clothed.

impulse *n.* a spontaneous force from within, often leading to masturbation.

incoherent *adj.* too afraid to accept that you're afraid.

incompatible *adj.* obsessing about one's "worldview."

incompetent *adj.* bungling. Calling a man this is the equivalent of calling a woman "ugly." It may be true, but it's impolite.

indecent *adj.* peeing in public, or looking as if you'd like to.

independence *n.* autonomy men give up in exchange for (1) a girlfriend, (2) a wife and kids, and/or (3) membership in the army, the priesthood, or IBM.

indirect *adj.* scared.

indulge *v.* to satisfy a craving, as for pizza, or for an eyeful of the Women of the Big Ten.

inevitable *adj.* unavoidable, like occasional war, frequent suffering, and false vows of love made to those who won't loosen their thighs without them.

inexpressible *adj.* incapable of being communicated. Men's real feelings will be inexpressible, as long as women are shocked by what men express.

infantilize *v.* to call a woman "baby."

infatuation *n.* the illusion that a woman's essence is as beautiful as her appearance. To remove the illusion, get to know her. If you still like her, it's "love."

infinite *adj*. boundless, like the love of Romeo and Juliet. Or like insect swarms; mailing lists; the catalogues spawned by mailing lists.

influence *v*. to convince through flattery.

ingenue *n*. a girl who wears a wide skirt around her tiny waist and manages to remain untouched and pure, without gaining any weight or perceptiveness, throughout the entire history of literature and film.

initiative *n*. fervor at the beginning. Fervor at the end is known as endurance. Initiative is easier.

insecure *adj*. feeling completely undeserving of love and attention you nevertheless crave. Can be fed by excessive criticisms, compliments, and comparisons. *Suzanne immediately felt insecure around anyone who knew how to French-braid.*

insecurity *n*. the fear that you are the world's least lovable person. The less you let this fear show, the more men will ask you on dates.

insight *n*. an idea revelatory to one person and utterly obvious to another.

insult *v*. to attack verbally. More enjoyable than hitting. Hurts a man most when you attack his favorite quality or his attempt to pass for something he's not. Like calling an intellectual stupid, or calling a Frenchman who makes grammatical errors in English a Frenchman.

intelligence *n*. the ability to know what's going on without asking.

interests *n. pl*. **1.** *love interests:* people you love and want to protect. **2.** *financial interests:* investments you love and want to protect.

infinite *adj.* without limit, like your desire for an attractive woman who doesn't want you to Change.

influence *v.* to convince through bribery.

ingenue *n.* a woman so innocent as to believe she's the first one ever to end up in that position on a casting couch.

initiative *n.* action taken against one's dissatisfaction. It conflicts with those who would rather pretend to be content.

insecure *adj.* feeling that you are what you do and that what you do is inadequate. Scientists have concluded that most men are right to feel this way, because they actually have no intrinsic value.

insecurity *n.* the fear of female rejection and male contempt. Failure to advance in one's career can lead to both.

insight *n.* the ability to see what the boss sees.

insult *n.* a put-down worth fighting over, unless it was funny.

intelligence *n.* a quality prized in a woman, if she uses it to understand, rather than ridicule.

interests *n. pl.* things you *want* to do, besides eat, sleep, and have sex. Collecting stamps, for example. If you have many interests, you are described as "interesting" by people who do not share your taste.

interference *n.* poking around in the lives of others in order to help them. Men are wary of interference because they have watched too many hockey games and believe it is against the rules.

interpersonal *adj.* pertaining to relationships between people and other people, as opposed to relationships between people and their dogs, their computers, or their cars.

interpret *v.* to bestow meaning upon something that has no meaning.

interrupt *v.* to cut off in conversation, like a pitcher who throws the ball before the batter is prepared. Many men have perfected this technique by playing so much catch as children.

intimacy *n.* **1.** the spice of love. **2.** what men claim to have a problem with when they are withholding love or sex. They really have a problem with love or sex, but would never admit that.

introspect *v.* a recently evolved verb, meaning to look inside oneself. It can be quite moving to watch a man introspect, although if he sees you watching he might stop.

intuition *n.* inner vision; uncommon sense. Women have cornered the emotional market on this one, and therefore dominate the Psychic Friends Network and the advice columns. Men have managed to parlay their more meager amounts of intuition into becoming management consultants.

involved *adj.* the best possible description of a relationship when you're not really sure what is going on. *Melinda thought that now that she and Steve were involved, they should go away together to figure out what was going on between them.*

irony *n.* when it seems life is an elaborate joke and you are the punchline.

interference *n*. inappropriate blocking, as of TV signals by clouds.

interpersonal *adj*. the type of skills women have.

interpret *v*. to explain that what you said wasn't really what you meant.

interrupt *v*. when preceded by "coitus," and followed by "us," a Roman form of birth control.

intimacy *n*. sex.

introspect *v*. to spend time alone, looking within one-self for the source of your deeper feelings, motivations, etc. An ability uncommon in men, since the pay is lousy and the sex is dull.

intuition *n*. fancy word for "hunch."

involved *adj*. complicated. *"Gee whillikers, Melinda," said Steve, "that weekend plan of yours is kind of involved."*

irony *n*. a sort of humor in which you say one thing and mean the opposite. *With hidden irony he said, "I am not a crook."*

J

jealousy *n.* a sweaty, irritable state that occurs when one confuses love with ownership.

job *n.* a thing that can turn into a career if you don't screw up or hit a glass ceiling. Flo Kennedy pointed out, *"There are very few jobs that actually require a penis or a vagina. All other jobs should be open to everyone."*

jock *n.* someone who sees life as an opportunity to work out. Usually has an impressive sex drive, unless steroids have been in the picture.

judgment *n.* a crucial quality that disappears in the presence of love.

justice *n.* what would ideally happen if the world were good. There is legal justice, moral justice, and poetic justice. They are not always the same, but it's reassuring when they overlap.

J

jealousy *n*. the excruciating feeling that the person you love has a mind of her own.

job *n*. a thing you spend eight or more hours a day doing, so as to keep the rest of your life out of debt.

jock *n*. someone with a complex body and simple desires.

judgment *n*. a crucial quality that disappears in the presence of alcohol.

justice *n*. what you tell the judge you want, when you're really after revenge. Also: something you come to believe in, when the woman who dumped you gets dumped.

K

kill *v.* to do away with, by violent means or benign neglect.

kinesthetic *adj.* touchy-feely. Women have a strong kinesthetic side, which is why we touch all the clothes in a store before trying anything on. Some people are more visual or verbal than they are kinesthetic. That is fine, as long as the verbal and the kinesthetic types do not marry each other.

kiss *n.* an excellent way to gauge whether he's a good lover without getting too involved.

know *v.* to realize without being told. *I just know.*

K

kill *v.* to put a person or thing where they can never harm you again. An ability rewarded in wartime, but otherwise frowned upon.

kinesthetic *adj.* having a sense of one's own bodily movement, position, or existence resulting from playing a sport, meditating, or scoping women.

kiss *n.* prelude to the nitty-gritty. You learn to linger here so she'll let you linger there.

know *v.* **1.** in the Bible, to have sexual intercourse with. **2.** to become acquainted with, to the point that no mystery remains. If "1" leads to "2," there's little reason to hang around. If you hit "2" first, there's no reason to go to "1."

L

LISTENING AND LOSS:
THE HISTORY OF THE GOOD LISTENER
AND THE PHENOMENON OF LOST WORDS

Recently, in the Gobi desert, archaeologists unearthed the remains of a prehistoric individual—a Neanderthal with a highly developed inner ear and traces of what seemed to be semicircular canals. Historians rejoiced: they had found the first good listener.

Many anthropologists argue the skeleton is female because its ears are so advanced for its time. Women have since dominated the history of good listening. Their feats have included many heroic acts of listening, especially since they were not allowed to give public speeches in many cultures. The listening was sometimes excruciating, for example as in the Treaty of Versailles when the women had to listen to the men drone on about their slow nego-tiations and know that they could have come to an agree-ment sooner themselves. Mrs. Woodrow Wilson got a break in listening three months later when she ran the country during her husband's illness, but she was too upset about the president's condition to note that the tor-ture of listening had ended.

While it is well-documented that women on average say more words per day than men, it is less well-known that women also listen more.

L

lackadaisical *adj.* lacking love and therefore exhausted.

One might ask how this is physically possible, when, say, a woman and a man live together, for her both to talk more and listen more—*at the same time.*

First of all: Who does she listen to?

Well, she listens to her partner and friends and colleagues. She listens to those she phones. And she listens to herself.

Secondly: Who listens to her?

This is problematic, because sometimes a woman will say words that go beyond a man's listening capacity. Those words, never heard by anyone but herself, become "lost words."

In some cases, these words are lost forever. But in many cases, they linger in the nether space between couples. She believes she said them, and he believes he never heard them.

Both are right. She did say them. He didn't hear them.

The phenomenon of lost words can lead to minor misunderstandings and major upheavals.

On a small scale, a man may ask a woman to "get to the point" when she is trying to make several points of varying importance, some of which he is on the verge of losing. Or he may feel overwhelmed by simple statements that he would normally understand. On a larger scale, he may insist she is crazy and did not tell him something she did tell him.

Couples must be vigilant to avoid such situations.

She should be careful not to exceed his listening threshold.

He should be on the lookout for lost words.

—*JLB*

L

lackadaisical *adj.* displaying passive aggression; helpful for avoiding fights over going to the opera.

laconic *adj.* speaking rarely but profoundly. Men have many laconic role models, from the Marlboro Man on upward. Women have had fewer and they are more remote—say, the Sphinx—so we have had to work harder to cultivate our laconic sides. It took women a long time to get into the space program because astronauts have to be laconic.

lady *n.* what you know you've become when people start to call you "ma'am."

lag *n.* an inexplicable delay in a conversation or personal appearance.

laid *v.* past participle of lay. Often leads to another action: eggs are laid by birds so they can later hatch; coffins are laid by pallbearers so they can later rest in peace; foundations of guilt are laid by loved ones so they can annoy you for an eternity.

language *n.* a system of communication that separates humanity from animals, adults from infants, and people from each other. As this dictionary indicates, it's miraculous these days if anyone understands anyone at all.

lasting *adj.* enduring, like faith in the undependable, love for the recently imprisoned, or a blemish at the worst possible time.

late *adj.* Not early. There are different degrees of this. Slightly late is when you think they might have forgotten to meet you. Very late is when you start to think they were in an accident. Abominably late is when you start to wish they were in an accident.

latex *n.* what condoms are made of when they are not made of intestines.

laconic *adj.* spare of speech.

lady *n.* a woman who is gracious when a man holds a door for her—and who occasionally holds one for him.

lag *v.* to straggle. A way to get others to do things for you. *Steve liked to lag behind when it came time to do dishes.*

laid *v.* past participle of lay. What every young man wants to get for Christmas.

language *n.* **1.** a way to sway a woman, to the point at which you will no longer need words. **2.** later: a means of introducing confusion to a perfectly good sex life.

lasting *adj.* durable, as the impact of the Beatles.

late *adj.* tardy. If you plan to be this in general, it is best to start off that way, so your tardiness will not seem a loss of love. *"But honey, I'm always late! Ask Sylvia, or Dawn!"* Also: what you hope your girlfriend will never be. It may be avoided: *See* LATEX.

latex *n.* a substance that blocks semen, syphilis, and sensation.

laugh *n.* warm throaty sound that can mean "I love your jokes," "I hate your jokes, but I was raised to be polite," or "I want to bear your children."

leader *n.* an individual with enough charisma for the whole group.

league *n.* any organization that encourages members to pledge their lives to sustaining its glory. Examples include the Ivy League, the National Football League, and the Junior League.

leer **1.** *v.* to gaze and drool at the same time. **2.** *n.* a sleazy smile that is unwelcome unless the leeree is in a particularly good mood.

legs *n. pl.* objects to be admired and hence tortured—waxed, shaved, depilated, tanned, freeze-dried, and moisturized.

lesbian *n.* **1.** what a woman who falls in love with women calls herself. **2.** what a man calls a woman who isn't paying attention to him.

liaison *n.* **1.** a person forced to run back and forth between two other people who are too stubborn to get along with each other. **2.** *v. to liase:* to make everyone get along. A chic verb found only in fantasies and résumés.

libation *n.* **1.** a serious drink. **2.** the pouring of a serious drink to honor a deity. These days, they don't make deities like they used to. But the drinks are still the same.

life *n.* **1.** a series of choices. **2.** an opportunity to grow and love.

laugh *n.* inarticulate sound expressing mirth or derision, but best explained as mirth. *"Oh," said Lloyd, "it's not your outfit—I was laughing at a joke I heard yesterday and only just now understood."*

leader *n.* head of the followers. What you may become if you are a very good follower. Or a very poor one.

league *n.* an abstract organization, above which float the women you most desire. *Forget it, man, she's out of your league.*

leer *n.* what an admiring glance is called, by one who does not receive it.

legs 1. *adj.* the potential to last. *"Does their marriage have legs?"* **2.** *n. pl.* parts of the body often covered by people who are cold, shy, or heavy. *"I don't know, but his wife certainly has legs."*

lesbian *n.* a woman whose rejection you don't have to take personally.

liaison *n.* a polite word (because French) to describe a sexual affair.

libation *n.* a polite word (because religious) to describe booze.

life *n.* **1.** a series of demands. **2.** an opportunity to grow and die.

light *n.* **1.** source of illumination. **2.** a term used to describe one's love, as in *"Lolita, light of my life, fire of my loins"* or *"You light up my life."* **3.** not heavy or ponderous. *Jan tried to focus on light spa cuisine.*

like *v.* to love a little.

limbo *n.* an in-between state, sometimes also known as agony.

linear *adj.* an argument that proceeds in a straight line. A person who turns the key in a consistent precise direction without jiggling it, never changes the subject in a way that makes you blink, and always puts the same sweater on the same hanger. Then there are associative people. It's easier for them to understand linears than for the linears to understand them.

listen *v.* to hear with care.

liver *n.* body part near the heart that is uglier and even more affected by alcoholic bouts.

loneliness *n.* a sense of isolation one can experience even if one is in a room with hundreds of people or in bed with one.

longing *n.* desire that goes on and on. And on.

loss *n.* the departure of a loved one, by death or ingratitude.

love *n.* a word to avoid like the plague unless he's already used it several times—and you have it on tape.

love affair *n.* a relationship so good that it has all the wonder of love and all the excitement of an affair.

light *adj.* not heavy or ponderous. What a relationship feels like when you don't have to talk about it.

like *adj.* similar to.

limbo *n.* an in-between state, closer to heaven than to hell. Sleeping together, without a regular appointment.

linear *adj.* the type of thinking that involves thoughts that connect. Such thinking is often scorned by drug abusers and radical feminists, who have either lost the ability or never had it.

listen *v.* to sit still and take in words and emotions, and pretend that all of them are necessary.

liver *n.* one who has not died. *This one's a liver.*

loneliness *n.* a "sensitive" way to describe the desire for sex.

longing *n.* nostalgia for the future.

loss *n.* the departure of a win, by weakness or ineptitude.

love *v.* to like a lot.

love affair *n.* a strong enthusiasm, as for a team. *Steve reminisced about his unhappy love affair with the Boston Red Sox.*

love at first sight *n.* when destiny places two people across the room from each other and arranges for them to find each other exceptionally attractive. How destiny manages this, no one knows, but dating services everywhere are trying to find out. Love at first sight is sometimes considered a superstition; people ask "Do you believe in love at first sight?" as if it is akin to believing in religious epiphany. Like religious epiphany, those who believe already experienced it themselves, and all others will have to wait their turn.

lowest common denominator *n.* a term good for explaining fractions or ingrates.

loyalty *n.* utter fidelity. An emotional issue. You can <u>look</u> at the girl in the skin cream commercial, as long as you're <u>thinking</u> about us. That's why we'll ask men what they were thinking during sex. There is a right answer.

lucky *adj.* a compliment one gets when one is actually skilled.

love at first sight *n.* exaggerated lust.

lowest common denominator *n.* the lowest factor that all members of a set have in common. For men, the ability to put out a small fire by urinating.

loyalty *n.* **1.** what she wants from you, once you've made a "commitment." **2.** what you expect from her, without any such formality.

lucky *adj.* what having sex used to mean you'd gotten. Now the lucky one may be a virus.

M

machocracy *n*. government by those who feel the need to show off.

madam *n*. a charming female pimp who can get into more trouble for selling sex than anyone ever seems to get into for buying it.

makeup *n*. a dissembling art invented by the ancient Egyptians that caters to female creativity and self-hatred in one stroke.

man *n*. a willful being who opposes what he loves and loves what he opposes; who can provide a pillow in the space between his neck and his shoulder; who despises vulnerability in himself but loves it in a woman; who shows his thoughts in his face and keeps his feelings in his heart.

marriage *n*. an excellent way to remove oneself from the indignities and atrocities of the dating scene; the process of reciting arcane vows so you can feel holy and reputable in the eyes of the church, the state, and the people next door.

marry *v*. to make your alarmingly slavish devotion to your mate official.

martini *n*. a drink popularized by James Bond. Since then, men have needed to order this drink, and women have listened to see whether the man asks for shaken or stirred.

martyr *n*. one who excels at suffering bleak tragedies. A talent that comes in handy during wars and legal disputes. On the plus side, martyrs do get to avoid confrontation. That and its poignant nobility have made women especially reliable martyrs.

M

machocracy *n.* what women call it when a country is not run by a queen.

madam *n.* a term polite of address, but not of description.

make-up *n.* a deception to which a man will object less, the more it is needed.

man 1. *n.* someone who protects what's his, knows how to please a partner, and either holds a job or doesn't need to. **2.** *v.* to take over and operate. *Man the harpoons!*

marriage *n.* state of being that gives adulthood a bad name. Just when you have freed yourself from one family, you are expected to jump into another. Then you must stay with the same woman for the rest of your life, even though she may become less attractive and may stop loving you.

marry *v.* to enter into a relationship with a woman in which you both promise never to leave or cheat.

martini *n.* mark of manhood, among the crowd that remembers Dick Butkus.

martyr *n.* a person who sacrifices present desires, trusting that they will later be repaid. Religious martyrs can wait until death; other varieties are less patient.

massacre *n.* the point during a fight when you say or do things you will never be able to take back.

masturbation *adj.* the ultimate proof of the old saw—sometimes if you want something done right, you have to do it yourself.

materials *n. pl.* building blocks of inexplicable importance to men. It seems irrelevant, when something has already turned into something else, to inquire what it used to be. But they will.

mature *v.* to ripen. The cruel irony of life is that women mature faster but hit their sexual peak later than men. They are therefore completely at odds with guys their own age, and are forced to look elsewhere.

maturity *n.* a state to attain as quickly as possible by emulating nearby grown-ups.

maybe *adv.* what men say when they mean yes. *See* PREFACE.

mea culpa *n.* Latin for "it's all my fault."

measurements *n. pl.* numerical appraisals adored by men. If he asks you for your measurements, only agree to share them if he tells you whether he's measured himself and what the result was.

message *n.* an important series of thoughts left on a refrigerator or answering machine. Perhaps women would leave shorter messages if men promised to finish listening to the whole message before erasing it.

massacre *n*. **1.** a literal slaughter. **2.** a massive victory in sports—though the term is not often used when the losing team is the "Redskins" or "Braves," because of the unfortunate echoes of Sense 1.

masturbation *n*. like nose-picking and journal-keeping, an activity hidden first from one's family, then from one's roommates, then from one's spouse. Cheap, quick, and safe, it can take you through many a dry stretch. *"What's wrong with masturbation?"* asked Woody Allen. *"It's sex with someone I love."*

materials *n. pl.* things that may help build or fix something. What a man needs, in addition to skill, muscle, and tenacity. A woman just needs a man with those things.

mature *adj.* in behavior and bearing, resembling a librarian. Until women go for librarians in droves, men will avoid appearing mature.

maturity *n*. a quality often praised, but rarely rewarded.

maybe *adv.* a way to avoid "commitment."

mea culpa *n*. Latin for "I did it, okay? So let's shut up, and move on."

measurements *n. pl.* figures useful when constructing a house, driving a truck under a bridge, and choosing among a variety of strip clubs.

message *n*. a way for others to communicate with you from a distance. Superior to a direct conversation, because a message is more easily ignored.

midlife *n.* a point when a woman realizes half her life is over, starts to experience hot flashes and cold sweats, and wonders if she has become a sufficiently deep and spiritual person. If she wonders aloud, tell her she has.

mind-reading *n.* essential telepathic ability. A talent to develop. It requires focusing on others and imagining their thoughts. Can make you a great guesser and allow you to please more of the people more of the time.

mirror *n.* the only objective arbiter of how one looks. Men who use mirrors a lot love their looks. Women who do, on the other hand, believe that they look terrible and keep glancing to see how right they are.

mission *n.* a long-term goal; a life desire; a sustaining purpose. Feeding the starving. Helping the hopeless. Seeking perfection.

mistake *n.* an educational experience.

mixed message *n.* the stating of one thing accompanied by the contradictory appearance of another. Part of the delicious ambiguity that keeps life interesting.

modesty *n.* discussing your achievements only in the guise of talking about someone else's, using the segue "That's so funny because . . . !" *Learning that Steve was a tae kwon do student, Melinda said with modesty, "That's so funny, because I'm a black belt in karate!" Steve didn't see why it was funny.*

moment *n.* a morsel of time during which epic issues are decided.

mother *n.* **1.** someone who loves you when you're sick. **2.** the parent who intuitively knows what size clothing to buy you even when you're not there. **3.** a woman who, because she knows you so very well from before you existed, can truly test the limits of your sanity.

midlife *n.* a time of crisis, when a man tries to live the way he dreamed of living as a teenager, but couldn't, because the women he wanted went for older guys who had money.

mind-reading *n.* a skill men neither have nor want. Paying attention to words is bad enough.

mirror *n.* the only inanimate object that tells you your socks don't match your tie.

mission *n.* a good thing to have, if you don't like your job.

mistake *n.* a screw-up.

mixed message *n.* when "no" may or may not mean "try again." Guess wrong, go to jail.

modesty *n.* quality of drawing little attention to oneself. Highly praised by those who want the attention that remains. *Steve thought that by mentioning the color of her belt, Melinda had given up any claim to modesty.*

moment *n.* the kind of time you can afford to live for, until you're married or in debt.

mother *n.* **1.** someone who thinks you might be sick. **2.** parent who can teach you why to be a man, but not how. **3.** a woman who once offered softness, but stopped when you were a little boy—if you were lucky.

muse *n.* one who inspires creativity by playing the harp, dusting, or proofreading. Unfortunately, making someone your muse can suffocate the relationship. Better to rely on impersonal forces as muses. Happiness, nature, rejection, early spring, fear, competition, revenge, and rent bills all have been known to help artists out of creative funks.

muse *n.* a goddess who inspires a man's creativity. These days she often wears running shorts.

N

nag *v.* to bother someone until they relent and do what they should have done all along.

napkin *n.* a cloth or paper dining implement, to be folded more or less elaborately depending on who's coming to dinner. Don't fold at all for hated relatives; learn origami for your boss's boss.

narcissism *n.* the feeling that if only you could clone yourself, you would finally fall head over heels in love.

natural *adj.* lacking artifice, effort, or social skills. *Melinda found it took extra time to make her makeup look completely natural, as if she weren't wearing any. Steve appreciated it. "You're so natural," he told her, after she had spent more time than usual getting ready.*

need *v.* to need. There are two kinds of need: the urgent kind, and the seemingly unnecessary kind. Some do not understand this and appear genuinely confused when they ask questions like, *"But why do you need new shoes? You already have seven pairs."* You need new shoes because they are new. Then there are "needs" (*n. pl.*) beyond shoes, invisible but pressing. *Jan now understood how completely Lloyd had never met her needs.*

negative *adj.* unfairly critical without knowing what the hell one is talking about.

nest *n.* home base, where the children get fed and watered; or, a basket of eggs with fluffy things and a roof. Also *love nest*: a den of quilts and passion.

N

nag *v.* **1.** to harass with insulting repetition. **2.** to harass with insulting repetition.

napkin *n.* a paper object you place on your lap, to catch the stuff that falls, and wipe the stuff that sticks. Men are encouraged to use the unsanitary kind.

narcissism *n.* the juvenile belief that no woman could resist your penis, if only she saw it. Rarely justified.

natural *adj.* the opposite of polyester. *Steve hoped she'd notice his natural cotton shirt—but she was silent.*

need *n.* a word that elevates a whim to a moral imperative: *"Lloyd, I need you to listen," Anne said. "You aren't meeting my needs."* In America, unmet desires become needs when they find a lobbyist.

negative *adj.* what a man is accused of being, if he tries to introduce realism to a conversation.

nest *n.* dwelling a woman wants built for her before her mid-thirties, in which a man will join her if the nest has color TV and a full fridge.

networking *n*. befriending people who can help your career. Women have hundreds of years of catching up to do when it comes to networking, having been excluded from dozens of all-male enclaves, such as social clubs, pro wrestling, and dinner parties at strip joints. But we do have the advantage of having more friends.

never *adv*. a word men use when they're being melodramatic, but don't mean. *Lloyd swore he'd never sleep with Anne again if she didn't stop being friends with her ex-lover.*

nice *adj*. a compliment that is often intended as an insult and will be taken as one.

no *adv*. the easiest thing to say when you're too polite to say what you're really thinking. In bed, for example, "no" may mean: "I'm not as attracted to you as I thought I'd be," "Your sexual technique is so bad that I don't think this would be fun for me," "We don't have any contraceptives, you lunkhead, and I don't feel like asking you for child support," "Maybe later, if you tell me how attractive I am and improve your probing," or "Never—you disgust me and always have."

nothing *pron*. a significant something. *"Nothing's wrong."*

now *adv*. an approximate time, meaning in half an hour or so. *I'm ready to meet you for dinner now.*

nurture *v*. to treat pets as if they were human beings, and human beings as if they were pets.

nutrition *n*. the science of eating foods that are good for you instead of foods that make you feel good; the art of making you believe those are the same foods.

networking *n.* behaving in a friendly way to people who are not friends, and whom you don't want to seduce.

never *adv.* a word meaning "not soon." *Anne asserted the right to remain friends with her ex-lover, and swore she'd never sleep with him again.*

nice *adj.* a quality men sacrifice for themselves, so their wives and daughters may have an ample supply.

no *adv.* a small word that may or may not mean "stop."

nothing *pron.* a lack of anything at all. "*Nothing's wrong.*"

now *adv.* at the present, meaning within four minutes.

nurture *v.* to indulge, or at least refrain from abusing.

nutrition *n.* when you eat the parsley that sits by the steak.

OXYMORON OR IDEAL? THE SMART BIMBO

This happened in a mental hospital in Albuquerque, New Mexico:

Someone had posted a black-and-white magazine ad featuring Claudia Schiffer on the staff bulletin board. Christine K—, a nurse, demanded, "Get that bimbo off the wall!"

Not wanting to lose the pretty picture too soon, a co-worker asked a stalling question: "How do you know she's a bimbo?"

"Well, she's not in that ad because of her brains," Chris said.

"No, of course not. But what do her brains have to do with it?"

"Nothing. That's why I want her off the wall."

"But how do you know she's a bimbo?" he persisted.

"You just admitted she's not up there for being bright."

"Right—but what does that have to do with it?"

"That's what a bimbo is. Bimbos are stupid. That's what makes 'em bimbos." She shuffled through the physicians' orders, confirming the meds for the shift.

"Really?" he said. He wondered if it was one of those words, like "indicted," that he had seen as a child and never fully understood.

"Yeah. What did you think it meant?"

"I always thought it meant a woman who was easy," he said.

observant *adj.* luminously aware of all around you, from newly styled haircuts to imminent nervous breakdowns.

"No. That has nothing to do with it."

Other women, nearby, agreed with Chris. They felt bimbos made all women appear stupid. The Schiffer ad was in trouble.

A male co-worker walked by. "Brian—what does 'bimbo' mean to you?"

"Why?" he asked.

"Because. I'm wondering. What do you think of?"

"Well, 'cheap,' I guess."

"Cheap how?"

"Well, cheap, like in a good way." Brian laughed.

"You mean they're easy?" the first man asked.

"Well, yeah," Brian said. "What's this for?"

The man called other units of the hospital, asking for the first adjective they thought of when they heard the word. Women kept saying "Stupid." Men kept saying "Sexy."

Women thought men liked bimbos because the bimbos were stupid. The unquestioned theory that men are "intimidated" by smart women had followed from this untested assumption.

That theory comforts "smart" women who find themselves dateless. But it doesn't help them get dates. Is a woman really supposed to act dumb?

No. Men are attracted to attractive women who seem to be attracted to them. That's all. Men hate rejection as much as women do. Smart, dumb—who cares, in the short term, as long as he feels warmth and respect?

To women, a "smart bimbo" is an oxymoron. To men, she's a nice possibility.   —BB

observant *adj.* quick to notice the key linebacker, even before John Madden has circled him with electronic chalk.

obsession *n.* an utter fixation on a person or thing tha fills a void for the obsessor, who generally doesn't have a life.

oppressor *n.* a person with a superiority complex whc lacks confidence in himself and therefore feels the need to colonize others. Throughout history, oppressors have lacked the finesse and subtlety of their oppressees, and have often been more overweight.

orgasm *n.* like an anniversary present, it's something you'll always get for him but he might not always get for you.

outfit *n.* a combination of clothes coherent enough to suggest emotional stability.

outlive *v.* the best revenge.

obsession *n.* a desire to possess so pervasive as to shut off the obsessor from outside input, even input from the obsessee.

oppressor *n.* synonym for "husband," "father," "doctor" (when male), "statesman," and any other form of "man" (with the possible exception of "garbageman"). A word that reaffirms the innocence and powerlessness of women.

orgasm *n.* a release of physical tension so profound as to often feel, briefly, like love.

outfit *n.* a military grouping.

outlive *v.* method Castro has used to defeat many a U.S. president.

P

Polite Forms: Etiquette and Customs

Being polite in the Female language means going to great lengths not to insult or offend the other person. If a man is ugly, it is best not to mention his looks at all, or to compliment his sweater when possible. If someone offers advice you would never consider, it's a good idea to smile and say you'll consider it. It's also good to smile thankfully when you are told things you already know; this differs from the male code, in which pretending you know things you don't know becomes more important. In fact, in the female code of manners, it is critical to smile a lot, until your face muscles start to hurt. That way, you will look more attractive, your manner will seem less harsh, and your success will be less resented.

In case your success is resented, however, it is good to apologize early and often. It is nice to apologize for successes and failures that were your sole responsibility. It is also crucial to apologize for things that could not possibly be your fault, like death and traffic.

Doing favors for others is considered good form, though return favors may not be forthcoming. Favors should ideally make those around you happy, but may only make them embarrassed to run into you. As the twelfth-century intellectual Heloise observed after her life was ruined by her great love and numerous well-wishers:

I am convinced by this sad experience that it is natural to avoid those to whom we have been too much obliged and that uncommon generosity causes neglect rather than gratitude.

And she was a nun. Things haven't changed much since then. But "uncommon generosity" should remain a goal, no matter the consequences.

—JLB

P

POLITE FORMS: ETIQUETTE AND CUSTOMS

Being polite in the Male language consists primarily of speaking differently to men than to women. Men continue to find that when they try to speak to women as they do to men, women are offended, whether the man intended an insult or a compliment. Men who do not adjust to this reality will be shunned by one gender or the other—if they treat both genders as they would treat women, they will seem condescending and effeminate to men; if they treat both genders as they would treat men, they will be in court on harassment charges. Unless they've spoken to a post-feminist, and then they may find themselves scandalized by what she says back—see discussion of Post-Feminist Dialect under "D."

Thus: men learn to smile more at women than at men, to discuss the appearance of other women almost exclusively with men, to stop in the middle of a dirty joke if a woman enters the room. Skill in following these guidelines unobtrusively will determine how well one is liked, which determines how much of one's way one gets.   —BB

P

pack *v.* to squeeze everything you own into a small suitcase before going on a trip.

pain *n.* **1.** emotional anguish. **2.** physical anguish. *See* BEAUTY.

pants *n. pl.* **1.** clothing to wear when you're feeling confident and want to be comfortable. **2.** short little breaths that you have to take when you put on a really tight skirt and realize you should have worn the pants instead.

paradise *n.* where Adam and Eve lived before their curiosity got the better of them.

park *n.* a romantic place to feed fantasies or pigeons.

parthenogenesis *n.* asexual reproduction. Simone de Beauvoir wrote of parthenogenesis experiments, "In many species the male appears to be fundamentally unnecessary," an alarming but somewhat comforting fact.

pass **1.** *v.* to not fail. *She passed.* **2.** *v.* to not irritate. *It passed.* **3.** *n.* an indication that someone wants to sleep with you, which may fail or irritate. *He made a pass.*

passive *adj.* how one controls a situation without seeming to, for example by manipulating seating arrangements or not returning phone calls.

patience *n.* the ability to wait around for endless periods of time in case life decides to surprise you, which it rarely does. Patience was once good. But in 1909, Charlotte Perkins Gilman said, *"There was a time when Patience ceased to be a virtue. It was long ago."*

P

pack *v.* to carry a concealed weapon.

pain *n.* a feeling that makes you want to say, "Ow." Don't, though, unless you want to teach people how they can hurt you.

pants *n. pl.* **1.** cloth, denim, or leather article of clothing with which to cover one's legs. **2.** noises to make, short minutes after the legs have been uncovered.

paradise *n.* a bevy of beautiful women. Failing that, a decent all-you-can-eat buffet.

park *n.* a fenced-in place to play baseball.

parthenogenesis *n.* development of the egg without fertilization. But why bother?

pass *n.* **1.** the forward toss of a football. **2.** the gesture of a forward person. Both moves risk a big loss, in hopes of a big gain.

passive *adj.* how men are able to behave while beautiful women come right at them—in their dreams.

patience *n.* what people urge you to have when they don't feel like giving you what you want. A woman may urge patience on the topic of sex, a man on the topic of marriage.

patriarchy *n.* a bunch of men who ride around in golf carts together; guys who hang dead animal heads next to portraits of themselves; a lot of kings named Henry.

PDA *n.* Public Display of Affection. A crucial test. If a man refuses to kiss you in public, he may just tend toward shyness. But it's also possible he's having an affair with the person across the street, or would like to have one.

peekaboo *n.* a children's game that involves hiding behind chairs, hands, eyelashes, and strands of hair. Sets the standards for years of flirtation to come.

people-watching *n.* a sport that involves sitting in an outdoor café and thinking of the lives you could have lived and didn't, as the owners of those lives pass by.

perfection *n.* when worries lift and bubble baths are possible.

perform *v.* to accomplish impressive feats. *She performed surgery while whistling the score of the Ring Cycle.*

period *n.* **1.** an epoch of history. *During the Mesozoic period, all was chaos.* **2.** a time of the month. *During my last period, all was chaos.*

persistence *n.* the ability to ask the same question a hundred times even when you sense the other person has no intention of answering it.

phallocentric *adj.* any society or individual obsessed with towers, horns, or archery.

patriarchy *n*. reality.

PDA *n*. Public Display of Affection. Most fun when you are young and want to show the world that someone, at least, finds you attractive. As you get older, you sense the danger of letting other men see your girlfriend aroused.

peekaboo *n*. a way to tease children, by pretending to abandon them and then showing up again.

people-watching *v*. an activity most men perform best when the people are women. A straight man who is not an anthropologist tends to watch another man only to wonder how on earth he won the woman beside him.

perfection *n*. when skirts lift and a bubble bath would take too long.

perform *n*. what a man MUST be able to do.

period *n*. something a man can never understand but comes at times to bless, since its presence means the absence of pregnancy. It does seem hypocritical, though, for someone to have one of these every month, and then call us "gross" when we burp.

persistence *n*. a quality often deemed annoying in public and rewarded in private.

phallocentric *adj*. what people who are not men call men. They think men are always preoccupied with the phallus, and build rockets and skyscrapers and Washington's monument in its image. Nutty.

pickup *n.* a come-on. *Phoebe thought "Your hair does wonderful things in the humidity" had to be the worst pickup line she had ever heard.*

Pill *n.* medication men claim they would like women to take, though they don't seem to like its bloating effects.

pizza *n.* what happens when no one wants to cook dinner. If you live too far from civilization to order one, you should reevaluate your priorities.

plan *v.* a future agenda, involving oneself and occasionally others. These others should be consulted in advance when possible.

plastic surgery *n.* a process to disparage until you're fifty—and then experiment with later.

platonic *adj.* refers to an ideal state described by Plato. Can apply to anything in its purest form: pure thoughts, pure friendship, pure cashmere. Platonic love, which has led to much tragic literature and sex therapy, has enormous potential. *Melinda asked Steve didn't he think if they broke up they could remain platonic friends? He said no. She said that was not the right answer. He said hers was not the right question. The argument threatened to turn them into platonic enemies on the spot.*

PMS *n.* a time of month when we blame everyone else for our bad mood. Men are worse off: they get irritable every month, too, but they don't know when.

poetry *n.* a proven method of seduction.

politics *n.* a useful subject when others have run dry.

pickup *n*. a truck featuring a flatbed. *As a young man, President Clinton covered his pickup truck's flatbed with astroturf.*

Pill *n*. an invention that has liberated millions of women from their biology, making it easier for them to live the life they choose. But let us not thank the male inventors—they were undoubtedly phallocentric.

pizza *n*. a necessary complement to beer, for those inviting guests to watch sports or help move furniture.

plan *n*. goal you will achieve in the future, if you still want to and don't die first. People with no plans simply prefer chaos to disappointment.

plastic surgery *n*. similar to makeup: we like the results, but don't need to know the process.

platonic *adj*. **1**. a type of intellectual love for which physical contact is a contaminant. Named for the Greek philosopher Plato, whose words still mattered after his body had started to rot. **2**. a rationalization from a woman who probably doesn't really love you, because if she did, she'd want you to kiss her. You get this point, even if neither of you has read Plato.

PMS *n*. something you shouldn't mention. If she has it, reminding her will only make it worse. If she doesn't, suggesting she does could bring it on.

poetry *n*. a few sentence fragments about love, with your lust-object's name on top. Works about half the time.

politics *n. pl*. a sport loathed by those who don't know how to play. Such people seem not to realize that to complain is to participate.

popular *adj.* so socially desirable as to be almost universally hated.

pornography *n.* an art form involving naked people, weak acting, and shoddy production values.

possess *v.* to have and to hold. And to snuggle.

possession *n.* can mean passion or visitation by demonic forces, though the two are often confused.

possibility *n.* something that might not actually happen, but then again it might, you never know. *The first time Suzanne phoned Len, she liked the sound of his voice and she realized there was a possibility they might go out, the possibility they might marry, and the possibility that they might have three kids in ten years; just as she was considering naming the third child Frederick, she realized she had the wrong number.*

post-feminist *n.* anyone who enjoys cooking but also earns enough to eat out a lot; who objectifies men but also marries them; who discusses nuclear fission while wearing micro-minis.

power *n.* something to achieve so you can downplay its importance later.

prenuptial agreement *n.* a contract signed between people who should trust each other but clearly don't.

present *adj.* **1.** not absent; nearby. **2.** *emotionally present:* willing to listen without criticizing, support without judging, and love without hesitating.

popular *adj.* men who become popular often have the vague feeling that they're not quite being honest. If they lack this feeling, other men will have it for them.

pornography *n.* the depiction of people having sex. What else do you need to know?

possess *v.* to own.

possession *n.* the thing owned. Stamp collection, CD, multinational corporation, woman.

possibility *n.* a much wider field than "probability," and thus a more fun place to play. *There is a possibility that you will get a seductive phone call from Laura San Giacomo, that the Red Sox will win the World Series, and that Rush Limbaugh will take a vow of silence.*

post-feminist *n.* a woman who has read Catharine MacKinnon but likes a well-made blue movie; who spends little time on makeup but always has Clinique; who grows a garden when she can but doesn't mind McDonald's; who will stay with a guy who calls her "girl" but only if he's got a great butt.

power *n.* the ability to do what you want, when you want to do it. Usually lost before the age of one and never quite regained.

prenuptial agreement *n.* a good way to test a spouse-to-be's love and patience. A pre-coital agreement would test the same qualities in a prospective partner, but might seem a bit forward.

present *n.* a gift that's more fun to give the less obligated you feel to give it.

priest *n.* a man who pledges to give up most everything and then has to hear others confessing about it all.

problems *n. pl.* dilemmas to be discussed.

project *v.* a psychological term for thinking that others have certain qualities only because you have those qualities yourself. Many inaccurate stereotypes of women have been created by men projecting their own qualities onto women: for example, the ideas that women are especially vain, inconstant, and obsessed with money.

prom *n.* an event of such heightened sentiment, it is the only time you'll ever even think about accepting a corsage.

proposal *n.* a suggestion of marriage, made as inventively as possible.

proposition *n.* sounds like proposal, but has an extra syllable and does not involve marriage.

psychosomatic *adj.* when mental considerations influence physical health. For example, when you get a sore throat at a public speaking gig, contract a mysterious symptom-free disease before a dreaded event, or develop an allergy to your spouse.

puberty *n.* a time when parental affection is an embarrassment and other kinds of affection are an obsession.

public *n.* a place where one ought to be even nicer than usual.

priest *n.* intermediary between a disinterested deity and a sporadically interested congregation.

problems *n. pl.* obstacles to be removed.

project *v.* **1.** to send out, as in one's voice. **2.** to predict future success or failure, based on recent returns. **3.** to ascribe a quality of one's own to someone else. *She was smiling back at him. Did that mean she wanted him in the way his smile meant he wanted her? Or was he projecting? He stopped smiling. She did, too. He decided he wasn't projecting.*

prom *n.* an event of such heightened expense, a guy can be forgiven for expecting a little extra from his date.

proposal *n.* **1.** in private life, a hopeful suggestion. *Lloyd made a proposal to Anne: what about living together?* **2.** in business: a firm plan, floated before stockholders as if it were open to discussion.

proposition *v.* to make a sexual advance. Most guys prefer to do this without words, using a sort of a physical implication. Some, though, say words are nice, and may suffice.

psychosomatic *adj.* when bad thoughts lead to illness. Examples include progressive blindness and the growth of hair on one's palms.

puberty *n.* when your armpits begin to smell.

public *n.* a group that cannot stand much excitement. Thus, you may not pick your nose, teeth, or other parts in front of it.

pumps *n. pl.* sensible shoes that cover any toenail polish mistakes, corns, or blisters. Sensible, that is, until one leaves the paved path and tries to walk in the mud. Then one starts to wonder why men monopolize all the really sensible shoes.

punch *n.* **1.** a tropical drink that may or may not come with a diminutive umbrella. **2.** a gesture used by men to hurt each other or demonstrate affection.

purse *n.* a receptacle that fits everything. Preparedness Central. A microcosm of a woman's identity. If you don't appreciate what's in her purse, chances are you're not going to appreciate her.

pumps *v.* what the young man does with iron, so he'll be able to attract targets other than his hat.

punch *n.* **1.** a good thing to spike at a party. **2.** a good thing to throw after a party.

purse *n.* the prize money at a sporting event. *The purse for this race is $1.1 million.*

Q

quality time *n.* what to spend with the kids when you don't have any actual time to spend with them.

queen *n.* a woman so powerful she refers to herself as "we."

question *n.* the most polite way of phrasing something, even when you already have the answer.

Q

quality time *n.* a phrase used by employers and ex-wives to make it seem we have lost little when we get one weekend per month.

queen *n.* beauty contest winner smiled on by Americans, who tend to find the other kinds (female monarchs, men in dresses) ominous.

question *n.* one of the least polite modes of address, if your tone of voice indicates you already have your answer.

R

rack *n.* **1.** a little shelf for spices. **2.** the place where clothes grow.

rake *n.* originally an English aristocrat who rode about the countryside deflowering virgins. Now a man who tells you his fantasies about sleeping with hundreds of women, getting into violent fights, working as a foreign correspondent, and dying young, all while wearing a leather jacket.

rakish *adj.* describes anyone who might develop into a rake. Rakish preschoolers wear dark glasses indoors and flirt with schoolteachers.

rape *n.* a crime women never feel the need to commit because we realize that forcing oneself upon others is distasteful and exhausting.

reaction *n.* an unthinking response. Sir Isaac Newton got really famous for declaring that for every action, there is an equal and opposite reaction. Like the laws of gravity, this is something any woman could have explained to any confused pre-Newtonian.

read *v.* to take in all aspects of a book or person, looking for meaning, symbols, and ulterior motives.

real *adj.* part of reality, as confirmed by more than one person.

reasonable *adj.* having the ideal attitude.

reassurance *n.* a commodity craved by the desperate and the hubristic. They will ask, "Do you love me?," "Do you love me now as much as you did yesterday?," and "Will you love me a few hours from now as much as you do now?" Reassurance should be given.

R

rack *n.* a set of antlers, or breasts.

rake *n.* an honest man, with more gusto than most.

rakish *adj.* a type of angle at which you may tilt your fedora, if you want to be considered a rake.

rape *n.* a crime for which convicts are sent to prison, so they can experience it from the other side.

reaction *n.* the word to use when describing a person's emotional response. Use "overreaction" only if you want it to escalate.

read *v.* to comprehend a person, a battlefield, or a basketball court and see where the weakness lies.

real *n.* the changeless prototype. "Real men" still don't eat quiche, unless there's nothing else in the fridge.

reasonable *adj.* what you should pretend she already is.

reassurance *n.* steady, nurturing feeling a man is expected to give during moments of crisis and calm, and expects to receive for the first two days of unemployment or impotence.

rebound *n*. when you fall in love with a complete stranger you met three minutes ago because you're still fixated on the person who left you three minutes before that.

reflection *n*. the process of turning yesterday's good idea into today's bad idea.

regret *n*. the long-term side effect of either excessive depravity or excessive prudence.

rejection *n*. **1.** the well-intentioned ousting of a person from your life. **2.** the painful ousting of you by a person with bad intentions.

relationship *n*. when he knows your bra size.

relieved *adj*. free of dread or obligation.

respect *n*. a quality women command if they dress conservatively enough. As Edna Ferber explained, *"A woman can look both moral and exciting—if she also looks as if it was quite a struggle."*

response *n*. what comes after someone has just paid great attention listening to you.

restraint *n*. the superhuman willpower you draw upon when you resist the urge to call him and wait for him to call instead.

retrospect *n*. a glow that enhances a phenomenon as actual memories of it fade. Capable of reheating love that has been frozen.

rebound *n.* **1.** the bounce of a basketball after a missed shot. **2.** the bounce of a person after a missed relationship.

reflection *n.* **1.** a manifestation. *The Lakers' success was a reflection of Pat Riley's coaching, as well as the abilities of the players.* **2.** careful consideration. *Lloyd found that his best time for reflection was when he was on the can.*

regret *n.* the long-term side effect of either excessive shyness or excessive marriage.

rejection *n.* a stinging denial, courted by those who try to shoot a jump shot over Hakeem Olajuwon, or a line of bull past Sigourney Weaver.

relationship *n.* a state she will assume you are in after two sexual encounters. Play along.

relieved *v.* what a man closing his fly has probably just done to himself.

respect *n.* a tribute many men would kill for, and may feel that they need to.

response *n.* an answer that shows your awareness that a question has been asked. For example, "Yeah, in a minute, dear," or "Huh?"

restraint *n.* a set of leather straps with metal buckles.

retrospect *n.* a place to which we must travel before we realize that we were wrong.

revenge *n.* befriending or helping those who deserve to be satisfyingly murdered. *Jan suddenly understood how she might get revenge, and called Anne to make a lunch date.*

reverse psychology *n.* the reason that a bear will only harm you if you shy away from being harmed, and a man will only adore you if you shy away from being adored.

ring *n.* finger jewelry with special traits. Once thought to have magical powers, now they just have insurance policies.

romance *n.* a state of wonder that resembles illness.

romantic 1. *adj.* perfect. **2.** *adj.* significant. **3.** *n.* someone who knows to say the right thing at the right time with the right amount of vocal modulation.

roses *n. pl.* lovely flowers that come with irritating thorns and superior symbolism.

rotten *adj.* **1.** inedible. *The food was rotten.* **2.** immoral. *It was a rotten thing to do.* **3.** depressed. *She felt rotten.*

rules *n. pl.* personal laws we form in our heads that get broken as soon as a good exception comes along.

run *n.* a glitch in pantyhose that comes with a lot of hurrying.

ruttish *adj.* lustful. Describes male sluts.

revenge *n.* seducing a woman who's prettier than the one who turned you down.

reverse psychology *n.* the reason a woman will share her body only if you don't seem immediately interested in it.

ring 1. *v.* what a phone does. **2.** *n.* an arena for boxing. **3.** *n.* a stain on a bathtub, or a shirt collar.

romance *n.* what you call it when the straight-up proposition seems fated to fail, and you fall back on indirect means (roses, wine, poems).

romantic *adj.* always striving, never arriving.

roses *n. pl.* pricey flowers.

rotten *adj.* the best kind of apple to throw at a car, as it makes the most satisfying splat.

rules *n. pl.* impersonal laws we form by committee that get broken as soon as the ref isn't looking.

run *v.* to rush. Men are not allowed to run from things (bullies, bullets), but are encouraged to run for things (a touchdown, the presidency).

ruttish *adj.* lascivious. Describes the sort of woman you would not introduce to your brother because he might keep her to himself.

S

SIGNIFICANT OTHERS

When a woman with a significant other meets a man, she generally tells the new guy about her partner right away. She seems to be reassuring herself. She's letting the new guy know that she knows she's attractive—but perhaps more importantly, she's letting him know she's protected.

Some of women's attention to relationships comes from a gut-level fear, a fear that the presence of a significant other—even just the mention of that person's name—soothes.

With men, as usual, it is different. Men have fear, too—but they do not generally believe that a girlfriend, or even, in most cases, a boyfriend, will protect them if they are attacked. Significant others are nice to have around, but they don't enhance a man's physical security. Quite the contrary.

S

sabotage *n.* **1.** when an enemy undermines you. **2.** *self-sabotage:* when you undermine yourself; more common and more disturbing. *In an act of self-sabotage that botched the hostage rescue mission, President Carter sent sensitive helicopters into desert sandstorms without checking the weather report first.*

sack *n.* a large, misshapen bag made of burlap or cloth. *Suzanne's mother assured her she did not look like a sack of potatoes.*

A man alone need protect only himself. He can even run from trouble if he wants. A man with a woman must stand and protect her—even if it was her full-fingered response to a leering stranger that got her in trouble.

When a woman meets a new man, she announces the existence of a partner within an average of 1.5 minutes after the introduction.

Men are known to hold such announcements a bit longer, but generally no more than five years. A guy who waits longer than that is bad news; he'll get no defense here.

Some people say men delay news of prior commitments for the simple reason that they don't want the new woman to stop flirting.

The same people say women who mention a partner don't really mean "Stop trying," but are actually throwing down a challenge. In effect, they say, such women are asking: "How much do you want me? Enough to beat this obstacle, bright boy? Show me, and we'll talk."

Maybe so.

—BB

S

sabotage *v.* to destroy; to subvert. What a man is often accused of doing if he tells the truth. *When Jimmy Carter admitted he had lusted after other women, some wondered: How could he so sabotage his relationship with Rosalynn?*

sack *n.* **1.** an action intended to stop a ball from moving too far from the line of scrimmage. **2.** an object intended to keep two balls from moving too far from a man. **3.** a bed. *"I'd like to get that waitress in the sack," Tony loudly told his friends, in case they thought him timid. The waitress quietly put salt in his coffee.*

sacred *adj.* inviolate, as religious beliefs are. And confidences. And time spent alone. And time spent with the prince or jerk of the moment.

sacrifice *v.* **1.** to give up everything for a man in the hopes that he will one day give up everything for you. **2.** to love so much that you give selflessly, expecting absolutely nothing in return. Except a little recognition. Or a medal. Or eternal gratitude—see first definition.

salesperson *n.* someone who pounces on you when you're "just looking."

savage *adj.* uncivilized; difficult to tame. A politically incorrect, unfashionable term. These days, savage women are called "wild," savage men are called "violent," and savage beasts are called "endangered."

scotch *n.* a drink that a single man may have, but that women don't go for till their third marriage.

screwdriver *n.* a vodka-and-orange-juice concoction popular at sororities; it works wonders on the innocent, allowing them to drown their sorrows but causing them to believe that they are having breakfast at the same time.

seamy *adj.* describes the underside of things, where seams show. Best hidden.

second base *n.* intent fondling above the waist.

seduce *v.* to decide to make love to someone and then get them to think it was their idea.

sacred *adj.* respected in itself; taboo, and thus undiscussed. A talk show in which a teenage girl tells millions of viewers that her mom is a slut exemplifies the death of the sacred. Previously, if your mom was a slut, you kept it to yourself.

sacrifice *v.* **1.** to walk on the side nearest the road, because you are accompanying a woman. **2.** in baseball, to bunt or hit a long fly ball in an effort to advance the runner, knowing you will probably not make it to first. **3.** to fall on a hand grenade, because your buddy has children. **4.** to keep a lousy job, because *you* have children.

salesperson *n.* what a man feels like as he approaches a woman for the first time.

savage *adj.* the type of violent passion you are expected to show for a woman, as soon as she says it's okay.

scotch *n.* what you drink, according to Norman Mailer, when you have given up.

screwdriver *n.* a metal tool that advances screws, and an alcoholic beverage that does the same.

seamy *adj.* the side of town where there is no need to sublimate sex and aggression.

second base *n.* **1.** white square equidistant from the first-base coach and the third-base coach—thus, a zone from which progress is largely up to you. **2.** twin projecting organs equidistant from the face and the hips—again, progress is up to you.

seduce *v.* to fool somebody who wants to be fooled.

segue *v.* to make a transition from one conversational idea to the next. The link itself may be invisible to everyone but you, but all that matters is that you see it.

self-absorbed *adj.* versed in the art of ignoring everyone around you in order to forward your own goddamn agenda. *Jan ran into Lloyd on the street and couldn't believe how self-absorbed he was; he didn't even ask how her therapy was going.*

self-esteem *n.* one's inner sense of self-worth, usually determined by the opinions of others.

self-fulfillment *n.* when you realize that the person who's going to make you happy is you.

self-hatred *n.* holding oneself in contempt. Not conducive to promotions or dating.

self-improvement *n.* Soul enhancement. A noble endeavor. Women enjoy self-help books, while men are more drawn to do-it-yourself books. We love the idea of fixing our inner selves; they love the idea of fixing broken household objects.

selfish *adj.* smart enough to pay great attention to your own needs but too dumb to notice anyone else's.

sensitivity *n.* a quality we crave most in those least likely to have it. *When Suzanne eyed the blood-strewn prizefighter on TV, she imagined him to be a man of great sensitivity.*

sensual *adj.* massages, mud masks, orchids, roasted coffee, wet sand, silk pajamas, all things that illuminate the senses.

segue *v.* to perform the next section without a break from the previous one. If you do this with relationships, the word used is "rebound."

self-absorbed *adj.* what you call a person who won't listen to you for three lousy hours.

self-esteem *n.* one's inner sense of self-worth, usually determined by the subjugation of others.

self-fulfillment *n.* something many men fail to seek, being too busy fulfilling needs like pride, lust, and gluttony.

self-hatred *n.* what you ought to feel, at least for a while, if you have done a hateful thing. It is fashionable today to try to get rid of our self-hatred, as it hinders us from enjoying our cruelty.

self-improvement *n.* the idea that you can make yourself a better person, by exercising, reading books, and going to the ballet. Whatever.

selfish *adj.* quality of accepting sacrifices made by others, but refusing to make one's own. Our society approves of the equalizing Golden Rule ("Do unto others as you would have them do unto you"), but not of its variants ("Do unto others before they can do unto you," or "Do unto others, then split").

sensitivity *n.* a quality prized in rich, handsome men. *Tony knew he could not afford to show sensitivity, at least not until he was famous.*

sensual *adj.* sexual.

sentimental *adj.* sensitive and weepy about life's important moments. Women can get sentimental about their child's first words, their third cousin's wedding anniversary, their nephew's pets' birthdays. Men get sentimental about their own birthdays and their favorite war memories.

separation *n.* the division of colors that bleed, spouses that cheat, and friends that aren't.

serial monogamy *n.* the natural state of humanity, according to anthropologist Helen Fisher; the practice of dating one person at a time till you're thoroughly fed up. As compared to dating multiple people, it requires more patience and stamina, but less thorough record-keeping and note-taking.

sex *n.* anything that gets you pregnant.

sexiness *n.* the art of seeming not to know how attractive you are.

sexist *adj.* when you base your idea that someone is incompetent on the fact that he or she is not the same gender as you. While the person may be incompetent anyway, this criterion is not a good one. And if she or he is competent, it may land you in court.

sex object *n.* a deitylike person whose sole purpose seems to be fulfilling the fantasies of mere mortals. Unfortunately, some apparent sex objects have other items on their agenda besides your fantasy fulfillment, such as doing their work, balancing their checkbooks, or shopping for riveting clothes that only add to their mystique and everyone else's despair.

sex worker *n.* the nouveau term for "prostitute," invented by people who wanted to convey that the sex industry is work. As if "prostitute" implies it's fun?

sentimental *adj.* a nice word she might use to describe you if you cry more than she'd like.

separation *n.* the gap between a shoulder and its socket.

serial monogamy *n.* a middle ground between the tedium of monogamy and the chaos of polygamy.

sex *n.* anything that gets you off and involves at least the thought of someone else.

sexiness *n.* the quality of reminding an observer that there is more to life than good digestion. It may consist of a bedroom voice, an off-the-shoulder shirt, or a glint in the eye caused by an errant contact lens.

sexist *adj.* when one believes her gender innocent of wrongdoing because it has been free of the type of power she wants it to claim.

sex object *n.* someone you only want to know biblically.

sex worker *n.* a social worker for men.

sexual *adj.* blatantly erotic, erring on the side of the obvious.

sexual harassment *n.* when the sort of intent grabbing you would love from the ideal man comes instead from a smelly oaf who determines your salary.

sexually experimental *adj.* this term describes people who make great lovers but are not necessarily marriage material. Just when she's hoping for a ring, he brings over the handcuffs.

share *v.* **1.** to give up sole ownership. A concept foreign to most men, who were raised to believe the guy with the most stuff wins. **2.** to open up one's heart. *Steve did not want to share.*

shave *v.* to torture your legs until they look just like everyone else's.

shop *v.* to fondle and consider thousands of objects before settling on the perfect one.

short *adj.* a word excellent for describing efficient meetings, lectures, and nightwear. Dorothy Parker explained, *"Brevity is the soul of lingerie."* If you are going to describe a short woman, however, it's better to say "petite." And for a short man, it's best to say "stocky," "feisty," or "clever."

shortcut *n.* a way of getting to the same place faster. Even if you get lost trying, it's bound to be more exciting.

sexual *adj.* good.

sexual harassment *n.* unwanted pursuit. Formerly known as "unrequited love."

sexually experimental *adj.* involving games of skill (try your luck) to be played with others at the same level.

share *v.* to distribute resources. A function poorly performed by the state in socialist countries and by the citizens in capitalist countries. *He did not want to share his sandwich because he believed it would lead to communism.*

shave *v.* to scrape your face until it's bloody and bald. An activity you long to perform, until you are able to do so.

shop *v.* something you do when you run out of food or when the holes in your underwear meet.

short *adj.* not overwhelmingly tall. Women who seek mates through the newspaper do not typically request a short respondent. Everyone patronizes you, and when you protest or show an ounce of ambition, they accuse you of having a Napoleon complex. On the plus side, you can hide in a crowd, can jump up when you punch—doubling the force, hence the success of Mike Tyson—and expectations of your endowment are low enough that you may handily exceed them.

shortcut *n.* a way to avoid the straight and narrow, masquerading as a way to save time. *Dad, let's take the Kings Road shortcut!*

shower 1. *v. to shower:* to heap or bestow upon. *He showered her with affection.* **2.** *n. bridal shower:* a party before a wedding, involving skimpy lingerie and lunch with the girls. **3.** *n. baby shower:* a party before a birth, involving skimpy baby clothes and lunch with the girls.

shy *adj.* terrified by human interaction, since it can be so catty, snide, and altogether unfair. Overcoming shyness involves accepting all of this as normal and sharpening one's social skills.

silence *n.* when you don't have anything encouraging to say.

silk *n.* one of the few things in life that is always superior to its imitations.

single *adj.* what you always think you are no matter what. Divorced people think they are single because they are no longer married; married people believe themselves to be single when they run out of things to say to their spouse; people in relationships believe they are single because they are not married. Real single people know single means them.

sister *n.* **1.** a female sibling. **2.** someone who feels that all women are female siblings and she is yours.

slip *n.* **1.** an annoying undergarment that has no sense of when it should and shouldn't be peeking out from under your skirt. *"I like your new slip, Jan,"* said Lloyd.

smile *n.* the one thing all girls are expected to wear.

SNAG *n.* Spiritual Neurotic Angst-ridden Geek.

soldier *n.* a guy with a mean crew cut, a great upper body, and a serious tendency to follow orders.

shower *n.* the world's most underrated invention. It wakes you up, massages and rinses you off, and remains always a warm, wet, private place to get naked.

shy *adj.* bashful. A skillful pretense if you have no interest in talking but don't wish to be seen as a snob.

silence *n.* the best sound during sleep, sunsets, Sunday afternoons, and some other times.

silk *n.* a fabric that may feel nicer than the skin it covers.

single *adj.* alone, unmarried—a state that makes men prone to depression and heart attacks, giving us that feeling of challenge we so crave.

sister *n.* **1.** a nun. **2.** a woman who gets her way by complaining that she never gets her way.

slip *n.* what you call a minor inconsistency, to avoid calling it a mistake, which it isn't. *"Sorry I called you 'Jan,' Anne," said Lloyd. "It was just a slip."*

smile *v.* what a man must do to reassure women who might otherwise think he's a stalker.

SNAG *n.* Sensitive New-Age Guy.

soldier *n.* a killer with a crew cut, into whom you may be asked to transform yourself on short notice.

solve *v.* to put an end to the fascinating and enjoyable process of analyzing a problem by eliminating it altogether.

son *n.* a child who becomes a man—how this happens, no one is sure.

soon *adv.* whenever one feels like it.

sorry *adj.* what to say after you've done something wrong, especially if you're planning on doing it again. Also said about things that could not possibly be your fault, you simply feel bad about them. *"My tooth hurts," said Lloyd. "I'm sorry," answered Anne.*

space *n.* **1.** the area around your person that belongs to you. **2.** *v.* to forget. *"I'm sorry, I spaced."*

special *adj.* a word invented for people with the tragic physical inability to say the "L" word. *If Steve told Melinda one more time that she was "special," she thought she was going to smack him.*

specifics *n. pl.* life's details. Women discuss specifics as a way of talking about the general. Men discuss the general as a way of talking about specifics.

spit *v.* to blurt out saliva or sudden confessions, neither of which anyone finds appealing.

spontaneous *adj.* all of a sudden. Also: *a spontaneous person:* one who is up for whatever contingency may arise all of a sudden. While most people pride themselves on being spontaneous, almost no one is.

solve *v.* to make problems go away, so we can get back to watching the game.

son *n.* a term of address, heard most smoothly from one's parents.

soon *adv.* before next week.

sorry *adj.* an expression of remorse. Being male means always having to say this.

space *n.* a domain free of intrusion. The more we feel we can get, the less we need.

special *adj.* **1.** available at a reduced price. *Our fried bologna is on special.* **2.** unique. *Steve almost told Melinda again how special she was, but stopped himself because he wasn't sure it was true.* **3.** what you want your bride to be, if you've given up on becoming it yourself. (If you haven't given up, you don't much need a bride, do you?)

specifics *n. pl.* essentials.

spit *v.* to forcibly eject saliva and sometimes mucus toward a target at least four yards distant, with accuracy to within three feet, minimal spray, and no drool.

spontaneous *adj.* unrestricted in emotional expression. Prized by psychologists, because spontaneous patients are more entertaining.

sport 1. *n.* anyone who puts up with anything. *Silvio tol[d] Jan she was a good sport for going to a party where n[o] one spoke English.* **2.** *v.* to wear. *Jan didn't mind to[o] much, since Silvio was being so charming and sportin[g] such a handsome tweed jacket.*

sports *n. pl.* what men talk about when they don't know each other.

stand up *v.* to screw up one plan by replacing it with another.

STD *n.* nature's way of telling you that a guy is a jerk.

steroids *n. pl.* drugs that supposedly enhance masculinity and strength by first making men look like pectora[l] superheroes and then rendering them impotent.

stomach *n.* a body part to suck in as often as possible—you never know who's watching.

stop *v.* something to yell at a thief or an idiot.

strength *n.* inner endurance that makes it possible to lose weight, overcome addictions, and have lunch with past loves. *Jan now had the strength to join the same gym as Lloyd's third cousin.*

stress 1. *n.* nervous tension. Also: stressful, stressworthy, stress-free, stressless. **2.** *v. tr.* to emphasize. *Suzanne's teacher stressed the importance of the midterm.* **3.** *v. intr.* to worry. *Having not studied for the midterm, Suzanne began to stress.*

sport *n.* a game-player. A "good" one neither whines about losing nor gloats about winning. A "bad" one is honest.

sports *n. pl.* substitutes for wars, as saccharin is a substitute for sugar (every once in a while, even though you know it's bad for you, you just gotta have the real thing).

stand up *v.* to blow off altogether.

STD *n.* **1.** sounds like FTD ("Florists' Transworld Delivery"), but instead of saying it with flowers, you say it with penicillin. **2.** a reminder of love. Even if your partner won't stay, this will.

steroids *n. pl.* extra testosterone, for the man who can't wait to be "huge." When you are huge, you attract more women, but steroids can make ejaculation painful. Better to keep lifting.

stomach *v.* to endure. *Steve didn't know if he could stomach another reference to Melinda's PMS.*

stop *v.* to cease. To withdraw and wait for the swelling to go down.

strength *n.* a physical quality little valued in the computer age, except at the beach and when somebody needs help moving.

stress *n.* the feeling that demands exceed resources, to which many men respond with denial. Shunning "hysterical displays," most men clamp down, drink, smoke, and clamp down more, until they keel over.

structure *n.* an inherent form of logic. Especially valuable when one is feeling dispossessed. *Doing step aerobics every Tuesday gave Jan's life a certain structure. It also gave her thighs a certain structure.*

stud *n.* a guy who could have his own exercise video but chooses not to.

student *n.* a person who is open to and willing to receive knowledge; who knows the difference between reading and skimming; who shows up in class and does homework on time.

stupid *adj.* incapable of grasping basic human nature.

subtle *adj.* delicate behavior designed to be more effective and loving than obvious behavior. But it doesn't always work out. *Suzanne blew off Rick in a wonderfully subtle way, by not returning twelve of his phone calls. Not understanding, he showed up at her house to tell her that her phone must be out of order.*

success *n.* a perfect balance of love, work, happiness, home, friends, relatives, health, beauty, fashion, society, good books, photo albums, and future plans.

success object *n.* someone whose most attractive quality is success.

sugarcoat *v.* to make something terrible sound wonderful and thereby please everyone in the vicinity.

suit 1. *n.* a business outfit **2.** *v.* to be apt. *"That color really suits you!" said Suzanne to Tony, desperately trying to think of something good to say and failing.*

structure *n.* the habit, whether a daily schedule or an addiction to alcohol or TV, by which a man covers for the loss of his mom.

stud *n.* a guy who calmly, quietly beds more women in a year than most men do in their whole lives.

student *n.* one who humbles himself in order to learn. If he learns enough he becomes a teacher and is able to humble others.

stupid *adj.* dumb. The qualifications change over time. Dropping out of Harvard was once seen as stupid. Then Bill Gates did it and made billions. Now those who stayed feel stupid.

subtle *adj.* the way a person may describe his own sense of humor if he has told a joke and no one has laughed.

success *n.* the best aphrodisiac.

success object *n.* a male sex object.

sugarcoat *v.* to sweetly lie.

suit *n.* **1.** something you bring, against someone you don't like. **2.** something you wear, to show respect to someone by whom you don't want to be disliked. *Tony was glad Suzanne liked his lime-green suit.*

suitor *adj.* a guy who's willing to wait around until you decide whether you feel like marrying him. Penelope's suitors in the *Odyssey* set a record by waiting for her for two decades. In the harried, post-epic world, suitors have less time, but you might want to try their patience for three years or so.

supermarket *n.* a place where people roam aisles looking at canned goods and each other, single people wonder what it's like to be married, and married people wonder what's it's like to be single.

supermodel *n.* a person so beloved by the camera that she can make in five minutes what a normal person makes in a year.

supportive *adj.* A crucial quality no matter the circumstances. *When her date confessed to her that he'd been raised by apes, Phoebe tried to be supportive.*

sure *adv.* a word that sounds a lot like "yes" but definitely means no. *See* NO.

surprise *n.* a wonderful, unrequested entity that manages to be just what you were thinking you wanted.

surrender *v.* to give in to sweeping, tumultuous forces like passion because it seems the thing to do at the time. Like losing the battle and winning the war. But in the world of love, surrendering is when losing means winning.

survive *v.* the main thing victims of tragic suffering must learn to do.

suspenders *n. pl.* a way men who have given up their artistic side to pursue corporate goals can express their vision.

suitor *n.* one who petitions or otherwise brings a case. Usually the case could be titled "Why You Should Sleep with Me."

supermarket *n.* a place to buy wine and look at melons. An easy place to ask an attractive woman for help—she may believe you need it.

supermodel *n.* a famously beautiful woman who knows how to communicate depth—except with her voice.

supportive *adj.* helpful. Just as her bra lifts her breasts, she wants you to lift her spirits when they sag.

sure *adv.* certainly. Sounds like "yes," because it is like "yes."

surprise *n.* the unexpected thing. Men like this in sports, less elsewhere. They particularly don't like it in the issue of their children's paternity.

surrender *v.* a fancy word for "lose."

survive *v.* the main thing dead people have failed to do.

suspenders *n. pl.* invented because men lack hips. Like height, suspenders can produce a great effect when worn with aplomb. Otherwise, they remind viewers of a clown.

sweat *n.* a love barometer; if you really love someone, his sweat is somewhat charming.

sweet *adj.* **1.** the way one is supposed to be if one is ostensibly comprised of sugar and spice. **2.** describes desserts that are so good that it is easy to confuse them with being loved. **3.** an expression of gratitude for inexplicable kindness. *"How sweet!" said Jan, when Silvio broke his little rule and allowed her to read the newspaper first even though she might crumple it.*

syllogism *n.* an argument that folds back on itself, confounding the basic principles of logic and the person you are arguing with. *When Lloyd told Anne they shouldn't marry so their marriage could never break up like his had, she protested that was a syllogism.*

sweat *n.* a work barometer. If you are laboring and appear to be in good physical shape, patches of this show up as an outward manifestation of grace. Otherwise, it reminds those near you that you are in terrible shape, or nervous, and may already have started to smell.

sweet *adj.* a quality lovely in a woman or a dessert. A book says it is actually men who are just "desserts," but this seems unlikely, as the demand for sweet men is rarely brisk.

syllogism *n.* a type of subtle argument to which you should pretend to agree, so you won't have to discuss it further. *Lloyd nodded gravely and said, "I admit it sounds like a syllogism, but I'm at a loss." He hoped that response made sense.*

T

TIME: PAST, PRESENT AND FUTURE
PERFECT AND NOT-SO-PERFECT

A note on the past tense and the future tense, and which makes us more tense.

When discussing their lives, women love to dredge up the past. Women do love the past. She will fondly ask him if he remembers the first dinner they ever had together. She enjoys reliving moments she liked the first time around—many times, when possible. He may become upset or feel threatened when she asks him. What's wrong with this dinner we're having now? he may complain. Why do we have to discuss a dinner we had years ago? Is something wrong? Nothing is wrong, except the progressive idealization of things that have already happened and grow more wonderful by the minute.

T

table *n.* a wooden structure upon which one can play bridge and under which one can play footsie.

tackle *v.* to hurl yourself into an impossible task and accomplish it. To overcome anything fate throws your way.

tact *n.* the art of refraining from telling people how awful they are and telling them instead exactly what they want to hear. Sarah Orne Jewett remarked, *"Tact is after all a kind of mind-reading."*

tactless *adj.* when you say the first thing that pops into your head without editing it out.

Men love to dredge up the future.

Where do you see yourself in five years? he may ask her, making her think he doesn't like where she is now or who she is now. But that isn't so—it's just his way of fantasizing that things could be better. He imagines that things that haven't happened yet could be better, as she fantasizes that things that already happened could be better.

So men are future-oriented and women are past-oriented when it comes to analyzing events. But then there is the question of *hypothetical* situations: the analysis not of actual events or goals but of "what if" events. When it comes to these scenarios, women can comfortably muse about the future: What if that guy made me pregnant? What if we had a wedding party of fourteen? Men prefer hypotheticals from the past: What if Babe Ruth hadn't played in the World Series that year?

In any case, one should never panic, one should simply pretend the other person is really talking about the time we would rather discuss. . . .   —*JLB*

T

table *n.* something off of which to eat, or on which to rest one's legs.

tackle *v.* to slam somebody into the ground as hard as you can, knowing he enjoys the sensation almost as much as you do.

tact *n.* what you display by not asking Joey how he feels, now that Phoebe has left him for an accountant.

tactless *adj.* saying to Joey, "Ah, you poor guy. . . . Next time, try H&R Block! Heh, heh."

take *v.* to ravish adoringly. *"Take me now," Jan murmured to Silvio.*

talk *v.* a way to make yourself feel better. *We need to talk.*

taste *n.* barometer for idiocy. *Anne had always wished she had better taste in men.*

team *n.* **1.** a sports gaggle. **2.** a group of people working together for the common good. Men who have played too many sports will say things like "we're glad to have you on our team" about hostile corporate takeovers or an efficient carpool. It's best to humor them, fostering something called team spirit.

teammate *n.* a person you learn to love, while learning to hate members of the opposing teams.

tease *v.* to make fun of. *Suzanne hated it when Tony teased her about her freckles, but at least it was a conversation.*

tedious *adj.* having extensive knowledge of one's intricacies and eccentricities, and a deep desire to share that knowledge.

tedium *n.* extreme boredom, commonly identified with a terribly unfulfilling singlehood, a terribly unfulfilling marriage, or life on a slowly floating glacier. To men, tedium is a story lacking a plot. To women, it is a story lacking a theme.

telephone *n.* life's central appliance.

tell *v.* to gauge something right away with startling reliability. *I can just tell.*

terror *n.* the feeling that you have permanently offended someone.

take *n*. the winnings. *"What was the take tonight, Silvio?" Tom asked later.*

talk *v*. a pale substitute for action.

taste *v*. to sample, as by sniffing and licking. *When Anne wore that red dress, Lloyd felt he could taste her from across the room.*

team *n*. **1.** a gang with a coach. **2.** a short-term marriage, to people with whom you don't necessarily want to sleep.

teammate *n*. a person you rely on to cover your mistakes.

tease *v*. to taunt. Out of bed, men do not like to be teased. In bed, then, they may assume <u>you</u> don't like it, either.

tedious *adj*. having daily anxiety about one's relationship and a deep desire to share that anxiety.

tedium *n*. boredom. *See* TALK.

telephone *n*. an easy way to avoid someone while seeming to stay in touch.

tell *v*. what you are not supposed to kiss and do.

terror *n*. the feeling that you have permanently attracted someone.

testicles *n. pl.* the seat of male strength and vulnerability. Once you understand that these are part of the same thing, you've got it made.

testosterone *n.* a hormone more present in men than women. Scientists used to say it made men aggressive and warriorlike. Now they say its absence makes men aggressive and warriorlike. All this shows is that scientists are as confused as ever, and men are still aggressive and warriorlike.

thine *pron. archaic.* means all yours, for all time, no matter what, even if everything else is falling apart, goddammit, in Old English.

think *v.* to free-associate.

three-day rule, the *n.* the feeling that if he hasn't called three days after your first date, he never will call. Trust that feeling.

tie 1. *n.* a bond between people. *Blessed be the ties that bind.* **2.** *v. to tie the knot:* to marry. **3.** *n.* that nice thing he wears around his neck when he wants to tie the knot or improve those bonds between people.

tomboy *n.* a girl admired for doing "boy" things. There is no equally jovial word for a boy who does "girl" things because boys do not get admired for doing those things when they are small, and that's when all the trouble begins.

tools *n. pl.* phallic objects that come in a box.

toothbrush *n.* the minimum packing requirement for a fling.

testicles *n. pl.* seats of occasional pleasure and a pain no woman has ever known.

testosterone *n.* hormone that lowers your voice and gives you the ability to shave. May or may not make you violent. But Margaret Thatcher took extra, just in case.

thine *pron. archaic.* yours. A good word to use in a love poem, as, "I pledge these two lips of mine,/ To those sweet lips of thine."

think *v.* to utilize mental logic.

three-day rule, the *n.* any pitcher who throws on less than three days' rest deserves what he gets. And that goes for his manager, too.

tie *n.* **1.** a contest nobody wins. **2.** a strip of cloth worn around the neck, as a noose.

tomboy *n.* a girl who can spend all afternoon throwing dirt bombs at cars.

tools *n. pl.* devices whose proliferation has paralleled the evolution of language, as men have sought to build treehouses, boats, and airplanes in which to escape the chattering of women.

toothbrush *n.* instrument for ridding your mouth of food chunks and slime.

touch *v.* **1.** to fondle with care; what you do to clothes you haven't yet bought or people you already possess. **2.** to spark an emotional reaction. *Suzanne was touched when Tony asked her to dance.*

tradition *n.* babies, aprons, a minimum of big decisions, gobs of time to philosophize and sweep.

trance *n.* A state of hypnosis or worship.

transcend *v.* to go beyond the ordinary and reach a higher, more spiritual realm of understanding. *Phoebe felt that her relationship with her dentist transcended mere teeth.*

transition *n.* an up-in-the-air phase between two sets of permanent, understandable plans.

translator *n.* one who negotiates several languages. *Donald suggested to Jan that she and Lloyd go to a translator to settle their differences.*

trendpot *n.* a fad-crazed vixen. Anyone who bought eight of Versace's monkey-studded metallic silver shirts as soon as they hit the stores.

trendy *adj.* when stupidity becomes crucial because it is the favored stupidity of its time.

trick *n.* an act of magic, performed by people who want to get out of a hole they've dug themselves. *"That's a pretty good trick," she said admiringly.*

trophy wife *n.* a woman so lustrous she can be polished and kept in a display case. Also, *trophy husband:* a man who glitters and smiles and marries well.

touch *n*. a caress. Not, perhaps, as critical a stimulant for men as for women. But it still beats listening. *Tony hated to dance, but saw it as the easiest way to touch Suzanne.*

tradition *n*. beards, tools, and unquestioned authority.

trance *n*. a state of comfortable detachment in which you may plan ahead without emotional distraction. Slipped into routinely by married men.

transcend *v*. what you try to do to your desires when you can't get sex.

transition *n*. an up-in-the-air phase between two longer-term partners. *Mary had helped him make the difficult transition from Betty to Suzanne.*

translator *n*. one whose job it is to pretend that two languages are equally important. The translator in the cold-war thriller *Fail-Safe* was a hero. Most translators, however, are not heroes, because it's hard to tell if they're any good.

trendpot *n*. a guy who had Air Jordans before Michael did.

trendy *adj*. a word best used while it drips with sarcasm. Like "bucko."

trick *n*. label given to a man by a woman for whom one-night stands are too long.

trophy wife *n*. a woman who knows her worth and has sold it to the highest bidder — as opposed to a prostitute, who merely rents.

tuxedo *n.* a suit worn by bridegrooms, doormen, and actors receiving awards. The one interesting outfit a man gets to wear, and most don't even appreciate it.

twerp *n.* a mean or irritating man, made more pathetic by his general unattractiveness.

type *n.* a category of people we supposedly prefer. We inevitably end up with other people. *Lloyd was not really Anne's type.*

tuxedo *n.* costume you wear occasionally to show people how you <u>could</u> look, if you gave a damn.

twerp *n.* an insignificant person, easily pushed aside. Weights and guns may help you lose this label.

type *n.* the kind of person who can evoke an erection. When a man says "She's not my type" it means either "I don't find her physically exciting" or "She terrifies me."

U

ulcer *n.* an illness that comes from worrying too much and not complaining enough.

umpire *n.* a ballfield counselor. Someone who can make decisions quickly and successfully wear black in the summer.

unbelievable *adj.* either wonderful or infuriating, because it could not possibly have occurred.

uncompromising *adj.* unyielding. A trait prized in men, loathed in women.

uncontrollable *adj.* when forces seem to be conspiring against you. The uncontrollable can be controlled if you learn to restrain yourself physically. *Every now and then, Anne had the uncontrollable urge to knock some sense into Lloyd.*

underestimate *v.* to guess too little because you can't conceive of more. *Jan underestimated the scope of Silvio's feelings.*

understood *adj.* the ultimate state of being, magically reached by patience, perseverance, and hard work. *I may be enduring a lot now, but one day I will be rewarded and understood.*

underwear *n.* intimate garments that tell a lot about a person. By looking at underwear, you can usually tell a person's hygienic habits, quotient for outrageousness, level of self-confidence, and taste in music. Of course by the time you meet someone's underwear you probably ought to know all these things already, but a little confirmation never hurts.

U

ulcer *n.* a badge of honor, of which a decent coach will have at least one. (The bad coaches get them, too, but don't tell that to your ulcerated man.)

umpire *n.* a referee. As neutral as God, but with none of His perks.

unbelievable *adj.* a characteristic that breaks the predictable order. *Before Nixon's fall, it was unbelievable that the U.S. president could be a crook. Now it is unbelievable if he is not.*

uncompromising *adj.* obstinate. A trait prized in battle, loathed in bed.

uncontrollable *adj.* what boys are genetically programmed to be.

underestimate *v.* **1.** what many a man does, with regard to the time a woman will need. *Silvio underestimated how long Jan would take to get ready.* **2.** what many an eager groom does, with regard to the power of his bride.

understood *adj.* perfectly clear. What nothing should be assumed to be, in a relationship of fewer than thirty years.

underwear *n.* **1.** a tank-top T-shirt, displaying chest hair. **2.** a pair of boxer shorts, briefs, or jockeys, displaying progressively more.

unemotional *adj.* lacking a moral base.

unequal *adj.* imbalanced, as in an uneven relationship. Take the raconteuse Scheherazade, who told stories to the sultan for 1,001 nights so he wouldn't decapitate her, producing a chunk of Arabic literature in the process. The sultan wasn't too anecdotal himself. This is the earliest instance of an unequal relationship that pops to mind, but there have been lots since then.

uxoricide *n.* a wife killer. Hopefully such a person can be identified before one finds the other wives in the closet. A good locksmith can help.

unemotional *adj.* not easily stirred or moved. How men like to appear. But men's groups are lobbying hard: they want "lust" to count as an emotion.

unequal *adj.* a relationship in which one person makes more money than the other—and is nicer, smarter, and just plain better-looking.

uxoricide *n.* a man who couldn't wait to be divorced.

V

vacation *n.* a time to spend with loved ones. Can also be a time spent seeking adventure alone, but you should always check the bylaws of the country to make sure women are legal there.

Valentine's Day *n.* a corny holiday when lovers give each other roses. While surprises are good, it is not a good idea to vary the rose theme.

vanity *n.* like worship of money, this is a quality that men project onto women. Men say that women are vainer because we carry compact mirrors. But what's vainer, really: acknowledging image is important, or pretending it doesn't matter while combing your hair in the side mirror of a pickup truck?

velvet *n.* the fabric of princesses, perfect girls with headbands, and formals on snowy nights.

victimology *n.* the science of being a victim. If you're a victimologist you do things like sue people when you trip. After a while, this gets tired.

violence *n.* a tendency toward destruction, developed by men who have not learned to communicate in normal ways. Women aren't interested, with the exception of certain girl-gangs. Most of us wish the girl-gangs would form girl-groups instead, sing some bebop, and stop reminding us of our disowned violent nature.

virgin *n.* double standard: you're screwed if you aren't, you're screwed if you are—and then of course you aren't. *Suzanne hoped Tony couldn't tell she was a virgin just from talking to her.*

V

vacation *n.* a time when you leave your work in the office and embrace the challenge of "chores."

Valentine's Day *n.* a holiday that is like an expensive way to renew a library book. (Less expensive, though, than letting it expire and then trying to take it out again, when others have been waiting . . .)

vanity *n.* the sin of loving yourself more than you love me.

velvet *n.* fabric worn by thin women in whiskey ads.

victimology *n.* the study of whiners.

violence *n.* an abusive phenomenon that will vanish on the day all women shun fighters and fawn over pacifists.

virgin *n.* like a new shirt—nice in some ways, but a bit stiff. It can be embarrassing to admit no one's worn you. *Tony was sure Suzanne could tell he was a virgin just by looking at him.*

virtuous *adj. Archaic:* practicing celibacy. *Contemporary:* practicing civic volunteerism, bargain-basement shopping, and safe sex.

vulnerable *adj.* having a soft, pureelike center. Most noticeable during weak moments such as childhood.

virtuous *adj*. monogamous. Virtue consists of opportunities deliberately lost, as opposed to those you could never have won.

vulnerable *adj*. an attribute men learned to fake while women learned to fake orgasm.

W

wait v. to wonder when an event will occur, and think of ways to seem as if you weren't wondering about it when it does occur.

walk n. a deliberate promenade. *Melinda and Steve decided they were good for each other while taking a long walk.*

want v. *to want:* to have a tangible desire, best expressed in simple terms. *"I want that"* is a good start, or *"I want you,"* or, more subtly, *"What newspaper is that you're reading and have you always been this attractive?"*

war n. the bloodiest way to resolve a disagreement. The trouble with war is that it's hard to be on speaking terms afterward, and speaking is so rewarding.

wax n. hot boiling material used in medieval torture chambers and in modern beauty salons.

we pron. **1.** usually refers to self and others. *We're leaving town.* **2.** can mean "I." *We're pregnant.* **3.** can mean "he." *We're giving up hang-gliding.*

weakness n. **1.** characterizes portions of the body or mind that can easily be poked, conquered, or won over. *Melinda took Steve to the oyster bar, looking for any sign of weakness.* **2.** deep desire. *Steve, it turned out, had a weakness for oysters.*

wedding n. a time to contemplate the nature of love, flirt like crazy, and consider life choices while wearing uncomfortable shoes.

weekend n. a time when love becomes more important than ever.

weigh v. to put yourself on a scale in order to gauge your social status.

W

wait *v.* to wonder when an event will occur and think of ways to make it occur sooner.

walk *n.* an ambulatory motion that communicates, whether consciously or not. *Steve decided Melinda was good for him while watching her walk toward a tree.*

want *v.* to feel lust toward.

war *n.* the last vestige of male supremacy.

wax *n.* one of the many places Elvis lives.

we *pron.* plural of "I." A good word to use in an argument, if you like the search-for-common-ground approach.

weakness *n.* a failing in yourself that causes others to love you or hurt you, depending on their mood. *Steve had read that Casanova ate six oysters a day; oysters had nothing to do with weakness.*

wedding *n.* ceremony through which you promise to trade your fantasy of many women for the reality of one.

weekend *n.* a time to do as little as possible.

weigh *v.* what you do to the merits of a proposal in order to reach a decision.

whatever *pron.* what to *say* to show you don't care about the appointed plan, anything would be fine—when you *mean* it ought to be dinner and a movie.

witch *n.* a woman with magical powers. Also a traditional label for any woman with too much power, magical or not, in history.

woman *n.* a most transcendent yet familiar being, who gives life and exudes vitality; who can do any work she wants and still smell good; who leaves an impression wherever she goes; who endorses peace but starts wars by accident just by being delightful.

Women's Studies *n.* curricula focused on the sociopolitical role of women, in which one learns that the reason women didn't dominate Western history was that men made laws forbidding them to do so. This should be apparent to people enrolled in standard history courses anyway, but is nevertheless comforting. Women who take such courses are gathering ammunition for inevitable *ad absurdum* arguments. Men who take them are trying to get laid.

womenism *n.* the highly unfair feeling that girls are more mature, prettier, and better-behaved than boys.

work *v.* to toil and toil till someone notices and is pleased.

working out *v.* going to a health club to try on risqué outfits, meet prospective lovers, and exercise a little.

wrap *v.* to adorn the outside of a gift and therefore amuse the person who gets to unwrap it moments later.

whatever *pron.* a word meaning "screw you."

witch *n.* a woman whose evil is obvious.

woman *n.* **1.** creator and sustainer of pleasure and life. **2.** person who wants co-workers to "be themselves" around her, as long as that doesn't include behaving like men.

Women's Studies *n.* a way to get a degree for using a really large vocabulary to hate men.

womenism *n.* *See* WOMEN'S STUDIES.

work *v.* to toil until you're <u>done</u>.

working out *v.* what you are supposed to be doing to a relationship problem, or to a body not yet perfect.

wrap *v.* what a man wants a woman to do, with a scarf around her neck, or her legs around him.

X

xenophobe *n*. one who fears people who don't speak one's language and who instead speak only the universal language of love.

X-rated *adj*. describes films that could once harm a woman's acting career and now can help it enormously.

X

xenophobe *n.* one who thinks foreigners are more likely than neighbors to covet his goods, his job, or his daughter.

X-rated *adj.* describes films that tell us everything we want to know about another couple's relationship.

"Y" IS FOR YES

I'm often asked by curious women friends whether men really think about sex as often as we say we do.

The answer is "Yes"—and more so.

Why is that a problem?

Other than work, sex is all we have. Our only connections to the process of life are to fertilize it, protect it, and feed it—you want us to fantasize about feeding?

Hey, maybe if our nipples worked. . . .

We have no blood or milk bond with newborns, and we aren't bred to connect with them in any other way.

We don't hold hands with our friends, and we don't

---

yes *adv.* what women say when we mean no. *See* SURE.

youth *n.* a time when one still believes it is possible to do everything and relinquish nothing.

"relate." We're new at this whole crying thing—but frankly, however healthy it may be, it's not that fun, even when you know how.

What's left to make us feel warm? Booze rots the liver, and we grow out of our basketball skills. If we don't have the faith of the Buddha, there isn't much left in this cold, hard world.

Looking at beautiful women, maybe touching a few—how can you begrudge us that?

The sight of a pretty woman gives life a meaning that needs no explanation. That's true even if she's not yours. Sometimes it's true *because* she's not yours. She represents life, and her existence makes you want to participate.

So don't worry so much if you see your man looking around, unless he gives you other reasons to worry. It doesn't matter where he gets his appetite, as long as he comes home to eat.

—*BB*

yes *adv.* yes.

youth *n.* a time when one still believes it is possible to do everyone and relinquish no one.

Z

zealot *n*. a guy too fanatically religious to worship only you.

zeitgeist *n*. a prevailing mood; whatever's on the mental fashion runways of the moment. *Suzanne wondered if her disillusionment with her civics textbook was just a personal opinion or part of a cultural zeitgeist common to American teenage girls.*

zone *n*. a postal or temporal district. *Tony seemed to dwell in a time zone of his very own, but Suzanne loved him anyway.*

zucchini *n*. a phallic squash.

Z

zealot *n.* one who thinks God is in a hurry.

zeitgeist *n.* German for "fad." *Tony just smiled, wh[...] Suzanne used words like "zeitgeist."*

zone *n.* place of mystical attunement, reachable by concentration or driving on a dark desert highway. *When Suzanne smiled without looking away, Tony guessed he'd be zoning by midnight.*

zucchini *n.* an inspiration.

e Arguments

THE QUESTION OF FUNGUS

JL: Bill, don't you think we ought to cut "fungus"?

B: (surprised) Why?

JL: Don't you think it's not working? Our definitions aren't funny.

B: Oh. . . . But other than that?

JL: Well—other than that, we don't need it.

B: Well—I agree it's not working. Okay, that's true. But it could work, don't you think? I mean, it's a funny word, isn't it? "Fungus."

JL: Well, I guess it's a funny word . . .

B: But it's not that funny, huh?

JL: (Polite pause.)

B: But I like it.

JL: (Polite pause.)

B: Okay.

(Repeat above, replacing "fungus" with nearly any word not currently present in dictionary)

THE CASE FOR THE CASES

JL: We should make the definitions consistent.

B: What do you mean?

JL: I mean the first word of each definition. Capital or lowercase. We should have agreed about it before. How does your dictionary do it?

B: My dictionary has capitals.

JL: Mine has lowercases. We should pick one.

B: Oh, but I think that's great! The fact that w
discuss it in advance, and came up with d
ways of doing it, and I know it's women who a
prefer lowercase, with the exception of e.e.
mings. I think it's very good!

JL: The copyeditors at Warner aren't going to think

B: Can't we tell them?

JL: I don't think so.

Lyn,

I got the package. Thanks. I'm incorporating the editor's notes, and will be talking to you soon.

Take care.
Bill

Dear Bill,

Did you read my note about collapsing "lonely" and "loneliness"?

I enclose a list of things for us to do, and those outlines I promised a couple of weeks ago.

all best
Jenny Lyn

Jenny Lyn,

I must tell you something about myself with which I am not pleased, but there it is: I am not capable of taking on new tasks until I am at least almost done with old ones.

I see the ideas you have for changing words, dropping those which seem redundant, and so on.

Yet, slow bull that I am, I cannot keep up. I need to keep doing what I am doing, the original task for which tomorrow's deadline was set, or I will feel frustrated and rudderless. I have a need to finish the task we set last week, before I can respond reasonably to your quite reasonable ideas.

Please: can we just do what we said last week we would do, and look later at the new ideas you are sending?

As always, Bill

Bill,

Hi. Please don't fret sweetie—I don't mean to be [throw]ing a lot of stuff at you. I find our miscommunicatio[n so] funny and genderesque, I wonder if we should exc[erpt] them in the dreaded "methodology" section . . .

If you had *read* the whole list, you would know that t[he] tasks aren't that great. I am sorry my letters seem "rathe[r] extensive"—I think the sight of them unread is much more overwhelming than what is in them. I do not think I'm having sudden new "reasonable ideas" but working on old ones.

(What makes Me feel frustrated and rudderless is the idea that you are Not reading what I have written to you.)

Jenny Lyn

Jenny Lyn,

Of course you are right these are not new ideas. I do remember talking about them. But they are new to me in the sense that anything other than dealing with editorial comments seems new to me right now.

That is probably confusing to you. I don't intend to make you feel rudderless. I do try to read everything you send me, but since I don't put it into practice right away things start to feel like they're piling up, and I start picturing you ready to send more, and wondering why I'm not keeping up, and why I am not sending you e-mail of equal length. And then I start to feel guilty in addition to feeling behind. And that makes the work, pleasurable though it undoubtedly can be, seem burdensome.

Perhaps you are right that this is a gender thing. I keep thinking of Linda Goodman's analysis of the Libra-Taurus interaction—the way the airy Libra runs mental circles around the slow-moving bull, confusing him but always charming, and nearly always right. And bulls do so like to be charmed, that they don't even mind being confused. Except once in a while. It's not easy for me to feel slow; usually I feel rather fast, by comparison to whichever verbal counterpart I am dealing with.

...ıg a productive evening, and appreciate your
...pect the trouble is less anything you are doing
...what I think you are expecting from me in reply.
...that is a gender problem. Also a residue of Irish
...guilt. I sometimes think my whole life is a residue
...Catholic guilt.

...ho, take care. Bulls may plod, but they have a
...sitiveness that comes in handy (inertia?), and I'm still
...gging away—

Bill

Bill,

You don't seem slow—I feel as if I'm lagging behind
too. The thing you said was premature I thought was two
weeks late and felt guilty for not sending sooner.

Your bull-libra imagery is great. I feel metaphorically that
you are trying to rebuild our house from the ground up,
while I am trying to sand and paint it . . . you think we can't
sand and paint it until it is finished, and I ask why we can't
do everything at once as we go along—then the house will
be painted already when it is built! Of course I am right that
we should sand as we go along or we'll have trouble doing
it later, and of course you are right that we should leave
some painting till the end lest everything drip on us.

Jenny Lyn

p.s. I've sent you a list of priorities

Jenny Lyn,

I was so happy to receive your letter about the house. It
was apropos, and showed you understand the situation
perfectly.

Thanks for the priorities. By the way, don't you want to
get the book in on time?

Bill

Bill

Yes I'd love to have it in too. Let's try not to see
a delay but an opportunity to give in an even bette.
on Monday.
Glad you liked the house.

Jenny Lyn

Dream

There were two women, it seemed a mother and daughter.

The older one asked, "Would you be interested in a dictionary for men and women—languagelike?"

And the young one said maybe . . . if there was a subtext of a young man and a woman—meeting—from two different planets, male and female, and trying to find a common language, because they secretly loved one another. Like they came from different countries.

So that you don't include every boring word—only the ones these two need at that moment —or if they wanted to live together.

They need words to talk about images of other men and women.

Of fathers and mothers.

Of people.